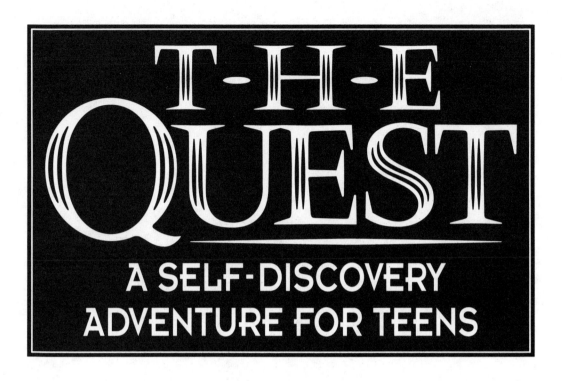

# T-H-E QUEST

## A SELF-DISCOVERY ADVENTURE FOR TEENS

Kevin Brown and
Ray Mitsch

A JANET THOMA BOOK

THOMAS NELSON PUBLISHERS
Nashville

Published in Nashville, Tennessee, by Thomas Nelson, Inc., and distributed in Canada by Lawson Falle, Ltd., Cambridge, Ontario.

Scripture quotations are from the NEW KING JAMES VERSION of the Bible. Copyright © 1979, 1980, 1982, Thomas Nelson, Inc., Publishers.

ISBN: 0-8407-4560-5

Printed in the United States of America
1 2 3 4 5 6 7—98 97 96 95 94 93

# contents

# PART ONE

## The Preparation

# Chapter One

## The Challenge

"You're just a wimp, man! You're nothing but a wimp!" A disgusted look flashed over Jason's face as if he were smelling rotten meat.

They were sitting in Jason's car watching a drive-in movie. It was one of those "slice-and-dice" films that John's parents would have hit the ceiling over if they knew he was watching it. Another friend, Bob, was helping himself to another beer and not saying much. He was off in La-La Land, probably because he had had two beers already. Scott was the fourth guy in the car. He was uncomfortable with Jason's calling John a wimp and came to his assistance.

"Back off, Jason. If he doesn't want a beer, he doesn't have to have one. It's his loss, and besides it leaves more for us," Scott said, reaching for another one.

John was being attacked by someone he considered a friend, just because he had said he didn't want to drink tonight. Yet he wasn't exactly sure why he said no, other than the fact that his parents would be mad, and he didn't want to get into trouble.

John was feeling more and more uncomfortable with his decision not to drink. What was so wrong with drinking beer after all? He didn't understand what he was feeling inside. It was as if he was being torn apart. He wanted his friends to like him, and he sure didn't want to be seen as a wimp.

"John, when are you going to grow up and act like a man—you know, do something your parents don't want you to do, just to prove you're not their little Johnnie-boy anymore?" Now Jason was hitting closer to home. John didn't want to be seen as something less than "a man," whatever that meant.

"Get off it, Jason! I don't have to drink just to prove I'm a man. When I make up my mind, I'll let you know. Until then back off!" John was putting up a pretty good front.

After he got home John sat in his room and thought about what had been said. *I need to grow up and be an adult. But how do you do that? There is no manual to follow. My dad hasn't explained what it means to be an adult. So where do I start?*

Too often, no one really tells you what it means to grow up until it's too late. Or worse, someone tells you what it's like to grow up while you are going through a crisis. Adults might say, "Well, that is what it means to grow up. It means making tough decisions about who you are going to hang out with." That's what they say *after* you get in trouble for hanging around with someone who could get you in trouble! You might think, *Now you tell me! Why didn't anyone say any of this stuff before?*

Adults sometimes sugarcoat it. For example, they might say, "Oh, your teenage years are the funniest and happiest time of your life. Enjoy it while you can!" And you think, *What spaceship did they just step off of! If these are the best years of my life, what have I got to look forward to?*

*The Quest* is a way to help you prepare for the future. Your mission, if you choose to accept it, is to find out about yourself and the world you live in—and to take what you learn and apply it to your preparation for adulthood.

Any journey can be pretty scary if you have to go all alone. No one cherishes that thought. Your quest is really no different. It is a journey filled with many obstacles and unexpected surprises. The nice thing about *The Quest* is that it gives you a couple of companions for your journey through life. John, the guy who stood up to his friend's putdowns, will be your first companion. Later, you'll meet another traveling companion named Beth.

So what does this quest look like, you ask? Let's look at one example of a quest taken by someone of international fame, Sir Edmund Hillary.

Many very experienced mountaineers dreamed of being the first to climb Mount Everest, the world's highest mountain, 29,108 feet at its peak. Some tried, only to fail. But on May 29, 1953, Edmund Hillary, a New Zealander, succeeded in conquering Everest with a Nepalese Sherpa tribesman named Tenzing Norgay.

It was no easy task. Months of preparation went into the operation, and many people were involved at all phases of this incredible quest. Special foods, equipment, clothes, tents, and many other important details had to be worked out before the climbers even set foot on the base of the mountain.

Then these rugged individuals finally started to climb. Day after day, with aching muscles, they pressed upward. Many times they considered whether the journey was worth the hardships they faced. Frostbite, lack of oxygen, and discouragement challenged them at every phase of the climb, but still they pushed themselves harder and harder, beyond anything they thought they could possibly handle.

Finally, after an intense struggle, they reached the peak and did what no person had ever done before. What an incredible feeling it must have been, standing there at the top, knowing their feet were planted in a place where no human had ever stood!

You, too, have embarked on such a quest. Behind you lies childhood; adulthood looms ahead. In the middle is the challenge of adolescence.

You're no longer a child and you don't want to be treated like one anymore. It's only natural that you should begin to be excited about leaving that phase of life behind.

On the other hand, you've not yet reached the point of adulthood. That is what this passage is all about, completing the difficult, sometimes frightening, growth and maturity process that leads to being accepted as an adult. Often, like Sir Edmund Hillary, you will wonder if it is worth the work that goes into it. But eventually you will discover you are much more responsible than you used to be and you are quite ready for the freedom that lies ahead.

This workbook is designed to assist you in better completing the difficult growth process that we call The Quest. It will be a spiritual adventure like no other you have encountered in your life. You will learn about yourself and the things you need in your walk with God. This knowledge will help you overcome the obstacles that could keep you from completing the difficult challenges that lie ahead. When you are done you will be better prepared for the freedoms and responsibilities that await you in adulthood.

The Quest is broken up into three separate stages that are similar to the stages Sir Edmund Hillary undertook. In the section called The Preparation you will take time to gather your resources, both emotionally and spiritually. You will be asked to explore the various sides of yourself and begin the adventure of understanding just exactly what you bring to this passage.

Next is the actual climb, the stage we call The Ascent. Like any climber you will begin to learn how well you have prepared for the challenge of adolescence and you will encounter some surprises along the way. Here you will reach a place of decision: Will you go back to where you came from, or will you keep going toward your eventual destination? Some teens never leave the mountain of adolescence because they find it more comforting than the many challenges of adulthood. Instead, they take their chances on the mountain.

Finally, the last stage is The Summit, your transition into the land of adulthood. In many ancient cultures children faced various rites of passage as they moved into adulthood. This passage is for you to symbolically show your progress into adulthood.

Every so often on this expedition you will find journal entries written by John and Beth. This is their way of sorting out their thoughts. We call it the Travel Log. You will be given an opportunity to record your thoughts about your passage into adulthood, too. After you are all finished, you will have a resource book of what you learned in your quest.

Here is John's first entry:

## Travel Log

*Well, I'm supposed to write down my initial reactions to this thing called the quest. I don't know how to write in a journal. I thought only girls used journals and diaries and stuff. I guess I will give it a try, but I really don't know what they are talking about. What is the quest? It sounds pretty bogus. According to the book, the quest is a journey that is supposed to test me to the max. It will push me to use all I have learned through life so far. It is a journey into adulthood. But what if I don't want to be either one? Actually, I don't know what they want. I don't know myself any better than I know anyone else!*

*John*

Now write yours:

**Date:** 6/24/96

    I am going to write down my most enter thooghts about this book. Well I think that it is going to be a real adventure trying to find out how I grow and change. Also how I have grown throogh oot the years. I am looking forward to knoeeing myself better

Mama

Now, if you're ready, pull on your hiking boots, turn the page, and let's get going. It's time to start your preparation for your expedition into adulthood. Your first stop . . . behind the mask.

# Chapter Two

---

# Behind the Mask:
# The You
# No One Sees

**B**eth, the youngest of a family with five kids, has always felt like the low man on the totem pole. She often came across as being really defensive because she was so used to having to fight for respect.

Beth would say she comes from a Christian home, even though her parents divorced before they started going to church. She really wasn't sure what her parents would say if they knew all she did when she was with her friends. She was able to keep things from them only because they hadn't asked her the right questions. Yet she felt as if she were lying.

There was at least one good fight a week between her and her parents about her friends or about who she was dating. Her parents didn't seem to understand her rush to drop everything to help her friends or her resistance to being part of family activities.

One Tuesday, Beth's mother started talking to her about her friends again, and Beth got angry. It seemed that her mother refused to understand Beth's side of things. After they had been arguing for a while, Beth blurted out something she later regretted. "Well, you certainly don't have much room to talk, Mother. You couldn't even keep your marriage together!"

Inside, Beth knew she had hurt her mom. Sometimes when she felt misunderstood she would lash out and try to hurt others because she felt everyone seemed so much older and smarter than she was and they always beat her in discussions.

Although she rarely admitted it to her family, Beth felt insecure. It was hard being the youngest when everyone treated her like their baby sister.

On the one hand, Beth didn't want to seem like a complete jerk by hurting others when she felt angry. On the other hand, she was afraid if she let her family know what was really going on inside, they would continue to treat her like the baby. Beth was one person on the outside, another person on the inside.

Before embarking on this spiritual adventure, it is important to get to know yourself. Some people have attempted this adventure believing there was no way they could handle it. Inside they felt weak and insecure. Because of this belief they only tried things they knew to be safe. This can keep you from trying the very things necessary for growth and maturity.

Others believed they already had all the right inner traits and thought themselves quite strong. Since they weren't too honest with themselves about their weaknesses, they became discouraged when things got tough, and they quit.

If you are honest about your strengths and weaknesses, as Beth started to be, you will be far better prepared for this difficult journey from childhood to adulthood. Until Beth could admit to being hurt and insecure, every time another argument happened she would continue to act like someone she was not. Everyone in the family would see her slamming doors and yelling hurtful things, and they would probably conclude that she had a lot of growing up to do.

On the other hand, by acknowledging that she had some weaknesses, she would be able to understand why she sometimes acted as she did. She would be able to admit to herself that she still had some growing up to do, and she would be far better prepared to look at the areas of her life that still needed work. Then, when life got difficult, as it always does, she would be able to look realistically at her weaknesses and work on them instead of trying to hide them.

The psalmist David knew the importance of understanding the bad points about himself. That is why he prayed, "Search me, O God, and know my heart; / Try me, and know my anxieties; / And see if there is any wicked way in me, / And lead me in the way everlasting" (Ps. 139:23, 24). David understood that being aware of the flaws in his personality helped him travel the right paths of his life's adventure.

So who are you? Let's begin by looking at how you see yourself from the inside. We'll call this your *private self*. Quite probably these will be things that very few people know about you, possibly only those closest to you. In fact, some may be things that no one knows but you. They will be thoughts, feelings, statements, even mental pictures that describe who you are inside. For Beth, this meant admitting to herself that perhaps she wasn't as tough inside as she sometimes acted outside.

## Working It Out

To help you look at your private self, we've prepared a simple exercise. Read the first sentence below. Write the first thing that pops into your mind to finish the sentence. Then do the same for the other nine sentences. Avoid physical characteristics like "5 foot 9 inches," or "blonde hair." Instead write what you are like inside, for example "I am someone who is afraid of the dark," or "thinks I am ugly," or "sometimes gets lonely," or "hides my true feelings." Whatever you write will be OK because only you and God know who you are inside. Here are some of the things Beth wrote.

I am someone who *sometimes feels more scared than I seem.*
I am someone who *doesn't want to be treated like a baby.*
I am someone who *isn't sure who I really am.*
I am someone who *argues with my mom a lot.*

Now you try it. Be totally truthful and list positives and negatives.

I am someone who *is lonely a lot of times*
I am someone who *wants more friends*
I am someone who *wants a little TLC*
I am someone who *tries to always speak the truth*
I am someone who *tries to love every one*

So, how did that feel? Sometimes writing about your inner, private self may be uncomfortable, especially if you have been taught that talking about yourself is selfish and conceited. This time, however, it helps you to know yourself and find things you may wish to change.

# Chapter Three

━ ━ ━ ━ ━ ━ ━

# The Mug Shot on Your I.D. Card: The You People See

*Something really weird happened to me today. I was talking to some of my friends, and they seemed to think I wouldn't have any trouble getting a date with Jennifer. I was sure Jennifer thought I was a geek, but my friends didn't seem to think so. I don't get it. Don't they see that I really make a fool of myself sometimes? When that happens, I just want to crawl under a rock. Jennifer was there when I stuck my foot in my mouth and said that Tammy was too nice to be going out with a jerk like Kurt.*

*John*

Have you ever considered how others view you? Obviously, John hadn't. It was quite a surprise when his friends didn't see him as he saw himself. Is that a thought you would rather not consider? It is sometimes pretty scary to think your peers see you as a wimp or a stuck-up snob.

At the same time, it is very important that you understand how others see you. We call this the *public self,* the mug shot on your I.D. card. Whether or not you are aware of it, how others view you plays a critical role in what you choose to do or not do on your quest.

How does this work? Well, let us give you an example. If you think people see you as strong, independent, and in control of your feelings, you are likely to behave that way. So let's say you are in a relationship with someone, and he or she does something to you that really hurts—like break off the relationship. The question you might ask yourself is, *What would someone who is strong, independent, and in control of his or her feelings do in this situation?* You will choose behaviors and even feelings to match this mental picture so that other people will continue to think that way. Everyone does this to some degree. God has created us as social people who desire relationships with others. One way to maintain those relationships is to match the picture others have of you in their heads. In this way, they will approve of you and continue to be your friends.

There is another side to this. Often you will actively attempt to fashion others' view of you. This could be called image-making. Probably the easiest way to explain this is to watch political campaigns. Most candidates have a press secretary, whose job is to weave an image of the candidate that will get him or her elected to office.

A lot of teens do that as well. They act in a way that shapes others' perceptions of them. That is what John had been doing. He had been working to establish a certain image of himself, and he was really aware when he blew that image. He was absolutely sure everyone else noticed it too and held it against him.

As you can see it all fits quite nicely into one complete package. You attempt to conform to others' view of you, but you also attempt to influence their view of you so that you can be perceived in a certain way.

Peter, one of Jesus' disciples, had the same difficulty. He is famous for denying Jesus three times (in an attempt to save his own skin) and he also was known to follow the crowd so he would be accepted. The story is recorded in Galatians 2:12:

> For before certain men came from James, he [Peter] would eat with the Gentiles; but when they came, he withdrew and separated himself, fearing those who were of the circumcision.

As you can see, Peter behaved one way when he was around people who insisted on strict conformity to certain regulations, but when they weren't around, he would eat with the Gentiles and do what they did with gusto and freedom. Sound familiar? Isn't that what we often do?

## Working It Out

Those who have been successful in the quest have taken the "bull by the horns" and sought to figure out for themselves how they want to be thought of and perceived. That is your job at this point in your quest. Ask yourself, *How do others see me?* It is pretty difficult to make changes without having some idea where you are starting from. You may need to ask some of your friends as John did. Here is what he found out:

Others see me as someone who *gets good grades.*
Others see me as someone who *is good in sports.*
Others see me as someone who *likes to help people.*
Others see me as someone who *is easy to get along with.*

John was amazed. His mug shot was quite pleasing. Now it's your turn. Be completely honest about how others see you.

Others see me as someone who *make good grades*
Others see me as someone who *good athelgi*
Others see me as someone who *is funny*
Others see me as someone who *can get along with almost everyone but a little bit of a smart mouth*

So what did you find? Do people see you the way you thought or were you surprised by what they said?

# Chapter Four

## The Hero:
## Who I Want to Be

John was daydreaming in algebra class again. That happened often because Mr. Cooper, his teacher, had a tendency to ramble on about pretty boring stuff. John was sitting behind Eric Blackstone, one of his good friends, and thinking about his own life compared to Eric's.

*What would it be like to be Eric?* John mused. *He never seems to worry about anything. Why should he? He is one of the most popular kids in school. He has his choice of girls while I sometimes have trouble even getting a date.*

John thought a little about Eric's family. He knew them from church. *They're pretty real, even if they are Christians,* John thought. *That's sure not like my family, who pretend nothing is going on, sitting in the pew so innocently, after dad gets all mad because we take too long getting in the car to go to church.*

John looked at the back of Eric's head. Unlike John's hair, which was wavy and unmanageable, Eric's blond hair was perfectly cut and incredibly neat. Eric was a much better athlete too. He was stronger and faster and had been picked as captain of the football team.

*I wish I could be more like him, then people might like me as much as they like him,* John concluded.

Have you ever compared yourself to someone you admired? Most people do once in a while. By comparing yourself to others, you are able to gauge where you stand and how you fit in.

The final part of getting to know yourself is to look at how you wish others would see you. We will call this your *ideal self* because it is the person you really wish to become someday.

In the previous chapters, when you listed characteristics of your private self and public self you may have experienced disappointment. Perhaps you thought, *That isn't what I want others to see!* Even worse, you may have thought, *This isn't how I want to see myself! What happened? How did things get so far from who I want to be?*

Some teens might wish they could be more like Superman, Batman, or Spiderman. These characters have incredible strength, power, intelligence, and other traits that make them better than the average human. That is why they are called *superheroes*. Unfortunately, they only exist in comic books or on television.

Other teens might mention role models or individuals who have done terrific things they admire and respect. A famous musician, a political figure like the president, a genius like Albert Einstein, a spiritual leader, or a hero who saved someone's life are all role models for others. They can even be people you respect and admire for just being themselves—a parent, a family member, or an important person in your life.

Often we wish we could have certain qualities that we observe in others. Some teens wish they had better physical characteristics. This might mean larger muscles, greater athletic ability, nicer hair, more height, more or less weight. This can be dangerous, though, because it can lead to unhappiness about the way God made us. David figured this out when he wrote, "I will praise You, for I am fearfully and wonderfully made" (Ps. 139:14).

What about your peer group? Do you sometimes look at others in another group and wish to be like them? Some kids seem to be surrounded by the "right" friends and appear to be extremely popular. On the other hand, you may feel alone or dissatisfied with the group around you, thinking you would be more content with more friends or "better" ones.

Do you handle your emotions well? Maybe you often feel sad, angry, or empty inside. You see others having a great time and feel that something must be wrong with you, or you feel you are missing something inside. You may wish others could see you as having it all together too.

Another source of discontentment might be your family. You may wonder why your family can't be like the ones on TV or like your friends' families. You might wish you could relate differently to your parents or siblings, have more respect, more freedom, better communication with them.

It is important for you to understand what you consider to be the ideal you. In the next pages, we'll help you list some of the ideals you have for yourself by thinking about people you admire, and then consider how you would like others to view you.

## Working It Out

In the space below, list some of your ideal role models (a friend, a famous person, your coach, a favorite aunt or uncle, a professional athlete, a teacher, anyone you look up to and wish you were more like):

1. _Elaine / Kim_
2. _Coach McDill_
3. _Mom_

Now think about the qualities you would like others to see in you. Here's some of what John wrote.

I would like others to think I am someone who _is confident of himself._
I would like others to think I am someone who _can make good decisions._
I would like others to think I am someone who _is intelligent but not geeky._
I would like others to think I am someone who _is a Christian, but still cool._

Now write out some of the ways you would like others to see you. This is your ideal self:

I would like others to think I am someone who _is respectful and curtious_
I would like others to think I am someone who _is very smart and knoledgeable_

I would like others to think I am someone who _/has a good christian back Ground_
I would like others to think I am someone who _is funny but loving_

Now let's put the private, public, and ideal selves together. Do they all match? If you're like most people, probably not. This can create stress and tension. When you feel one way inside, when others see you a second way, and when you really want to be someone totally different from either of these two selves, you can get very confused about who you are. To clear this up, you must begin by asking yourself, *Why don't my three selves match? Am I acting like someone I'm not? Are my ideals set too high so I can never reach them? Are there things I'm so embarrassed or ashamed about that I could never let anyone know?*

John saw three reasons why his private, public, and ideal selves didn't match:

1. *My private feelings are sometimes too embarrassing to let others see.*
2. *I show others only the tough and secure parts of my personality.*
3. *I'm afraid I'll never reach my ideals, so I hardly ever tell anyone about that part of myself.*

Beth had different reasons:

1. *I don't want to let anyone see that I sometimes feel like a baby.*
2. *I act angry and mean because that is how I stand up for myself.*
3. *My ideal is my sister, and if she knew she would think she was even more important than she already believes she is.*

Look back over what you wrote about your private, public, and ideal selves and list three reasons why these three parts of yourself are so different.

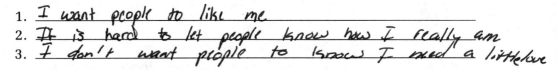

1. _I want people to like me_
2. _It is hard to let people know how I really am_
3. _I don't want people to know I need a little love_

Next think about what you can do to make these parts fit more closely together to minimize one possible source of stress and problems on your quest.

Do you need to be more honest with others about what is
      going on inside?  ☑ yes  ☐ no
Are you acting like one person outside but feeling like another
      person inside?  ☑ yes  ☐ no
Is your ideal self too difficult a person to be?  ☐ yes  ☑ no

Use the answers to these questions to help you think of some things
you could do to make these parts of yourself fit together better. John had
some pretty good ideas. He said:

*I could let certain people know just what I am like inside. I guess
sometimes I don't have to act so tough and could be more like my private
self. I also could stop trying to live up to Eric's good points and be more accepting of myself rather than trying to be an ideal I probably never will be.*

While Beth took a little longer to come up with hers, they were just
as solid. She wrote:

*I could accept the fact that I am the youngest and stop trying to show
everyone I am more mature than I really am by arguing and being mean
when I get hurt. If I were more honest about that, I might even be able to let
my sister know I admire her instead of feeling so insecure about it.*

Now it's your turn to think of ways to make these parts of yourself fit
together better.

*I could be more open to people
and let them get to know me. Also instead
of arguing I could just take it and go
on. I should also watch what I
say to others. Think*

This may have been the first time you've ever written out who you
really wish to be. After doing this exercise John decided, *maybe if I could
stop worrying about whether people like me or not, life would be easier.
Maybe I just need to be more honest about who I really am inside and stop
worrying if people will accept me.*

# Chapter Five

---

# The Personal Coat of Arms

It has been said that a picture is worth a thousand words. To make your quest more meaningful, we will sometimes ask you to draw a picture. The drawing doesn't have to be perfect, so don't worry if you're not a great artist.

The first project is a personal coat of arms. Many families have a coat of arms, a shield with pictures that represent the family's heritage and background. Your personal coat of arms will translate in pictures what you wrote about your private, public, and ideal selves in the previous chapters.

Think of a picture that represents the words you wrote in these sections. A word like *sad* might become a frowning face. *Strong* could become a barbell or weights. *Lonely* could even be a stick figure standing apart from a crowd of other stick figures.

Here is John's personal coat of arms. He used clip art and some magazine drawings. You could do the same.

This is how John explained his coat of arms:

*I began with the person no one sees. He is worried, sometimes even panicky about life, and he feels as if a storm is building inside of him. The* person I allow other people to see is confident and helps keep the peace be-tween his friends, as a police officer might do. I like to help others. I am sometimes a clown, and generally I try to keep a smile on my face. The person I want to be is someone who is strong like a lion. I want to be the best in everything I do. I also want to keep my cool in every situation. That is why I chose the sun; he looks as if nothing would faze him. That's about it for my coat of arms.

Now take time to create your own personal coat of arms. The most important thing is to make it meaningful to you—and to enjoy yourself.

# PERSONAL COAT OF ARMS

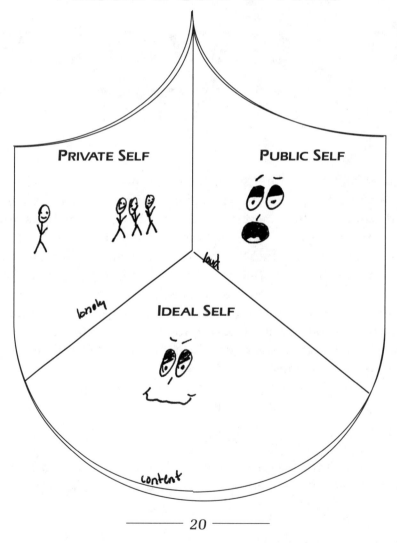

# John's Coat of Arms

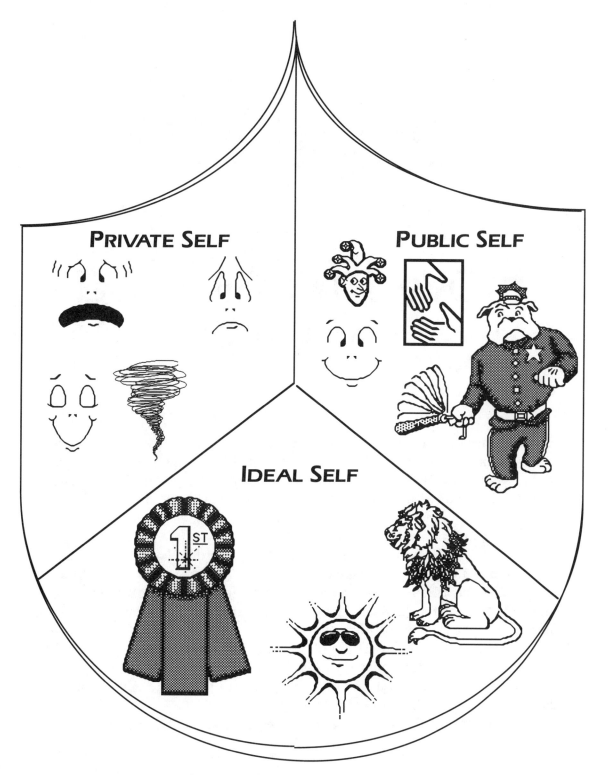

Private Self

Public Self

Ideal Self

# Chapter Six

## How I Think God Sees Me

**J**ohn sat quietly in his room. It was completely dark and music was playing softly in the background. All John knew was that he felt awful and he really didn't know why. He knew he had done OK during school that day, no major catastrophes or anything. He just felt bad. He was jolted out of his thoughts by the phone ringing.

"Hello," John said numbly.

"Hi, John. How is it going?" It was Abby, a girl he had met at a football game two weeks ago. They had traded phone numbers and promised to get together later. He had left a message on her answering machine almost three nights ago and she hadn't returned his phone call. It was just another reminder of the state of his life.

"Hi, Abby. Did you get my phone call?" John was expecting a denial.

"Yep. I sure did. I'm sorry I didn't call you sooner, but we were out of town all weekend. This was my first chance to call you back." Abby sounded happy and carefree. How did she do it?

They talked about the usual mundane stuff—school and mutual

friends. Just before their conversation ended Abby asked, "John, are you OK? You don't sound too good. What's up?"

"Oh, I don't know. I just feel down today. I don't know why and that bugs me," John said. "Abby, do you ever think about God much? I mean, if you don't want to answer that you don't have to. I was just wondering." John knew he was on safe ground. He already knew that Abby had the same kind of family he did, the parents-go-to-church-and-drag-the-kids-along kind of family.

"Yeah, sometimes I do. Not much though. I guess I don't see God as someone who is concerned about me. All the other stuff He has to do seems a lot more important." Abby seemed to capture exactly what John was feeling. It was weird how she felt just like he did.

Are these familiar thoughts to you? John and Abby are really no different from a lot of other teens. Most really don't think about God and how He sees them. God seems real to their parents, but they can't say the same for themselves.

John sees God as someone to go to in times of trouble, but the rest of life really doesn't need to have God in it. He hasn't given much thought to how he has come to this conclusion. Somehow in the back of his mind he feels that God frowns on a good time and only keeps track of the bad stuff he does.

Some teens think God doesn't exist or that He is just too enormous to know; so they say to themselves, *Why bother?* Others are convinced that God is intensely interested in them and wants a relationship with them more than they can even begin to imagine.

How God views you is a critical element in your quest into adulthood. Why, you ask? Have you ever tried to accomplish something that seems impossible to do, but because you know someone is behind you, believing in you and loving you, you find the courage to complete the job?

A number of factors influence how you think God views you. The first is a sort of boomerang effect. If you feel bad about yourself as a person, then you are most likely to assume that God feels the same as you do; you probably can't imagine anyone who really knows you feeling any other way.

If, on some of your better days, you feel OK about yourself as a person, then you probably feel that God really does love you. Notice that how you feel about yourself is quite conditional; it is only based on whether you behave in a way that other people approve of. If you really think about it then, you actually make God in your own image.

Another factor influences how you believe God feels about you: Your view of Him as your Father. One's understanding of a father is largely determined by his or her own father. So if you have a father who is loving, attentive, and tries to respect you, you are more likely to view God in the same way. On the other hand, if you have a father who is distant, cold, demanding, and critical, you probably are going to see God in that way too.

In the following pages, we'll lead you through some exercises that will help you examine more closely how you think God sees you.

## Working It Out

In the spaces below, write out how you think God sees you. Remember, don't put down what your parents have told you or what you think you are "supposed" to say. Be totally, brutally honest. No one is going to read this except you. Here are a few of John's responses:

God sees me as someone who _feels lost._
God sees me as someone who _really isn't going to amount to much in his life._
God sees me as someone who _doesn't think too much about Him._
God sees me as someone who _only comes to Him when I need something._

Now take some time and try it yourself.

God sees me as someone who _____

God sees me as someone who _____

God sees me as someone who _____

God sees me as someone who _____

God sees me as someone who _____

Based on what you have just written, what can you conclude about how you think God sees you? Below, check the qualities you believe God sees when He looks at you.

☐ A failure      ☐ Dense      ☐ Moody
☐ A success      ☐ Dull      ☐ Inconsistent
☐ Important      ☐ A geek      ☐ Confident
☐ Worth dying for      ☐ Stupid      ☐ Self-assured
☐ Attractive      ☐ Worth loving      ☐ Cheerful
☐ Ugly      ☐ Arrogant      ☐ Encouraging
☐ Smart      ☐ Proud      ☐ Optimistic
☐ Dumb      ☐ A snob      ☐ Assertive
☐ Fearful      ☐ Hurting      ☐ Aggressive
☐ Loves God      ☐ Hiding under a mask      ☐ Impulsive
☐ Confused      ☐ Loved by others      ☐ Sad
☐ Worthless      ☐ Cocky      ☐ Pushy
☐ Mixed-up      ☐ Conceited

Now look back over the qualities you checked. Were most of them negative, positive, or a mix of the two?

☐ Negative      ☐ Positive      ☐ A mixture

This answer will be important in the next part of the quest. So store it away for now. You will need it later.

Finally, take a little time and imagine what it would be like if you had someone in your life who believed in you no matter what, someone who supported you in everything you did, whether you did well or not. What do you suppose you would be able to accomplish? How do your feelings distort your picture of God? Let your mind roam for a minute, then use your Travel Log to record your thoughts and feelings. Here's what John wrote:

## Travel Log

*Something really great happened to me. I decided to help out with the school play called* Hello Dolly *by being a stage manager. I was hesitant at first, but my friend talked me into it. She said I would be terrific at the job, and they needed someone to do it for them. It turned out great! I had a lot of fun, and learned a lot in the process. It really felt good to have my friend believe in me that way. I don't think I would have done it if it hadn't been for her belief that I could do it.*

*I wonder if that is how God believes in me. It's hard to believe that someone as infinite and all-powerful as God would actually think about me—a tiny speck in this universe—and even believe in me in spite of how I feel about myself.*

*John*

Now it's your turn. What thoughts or feelings can you jot down about how you think God sees you?

## Date: _____

_____

_____

_____

_____

_____

_____

_____

_____

_____

_____

_____

_____

_____

_____

_____

_____

# Chapter Seven

———————————

# What God Actually Sees

**J**ohn was feeling down. It felt as if everyone had abandoned him. All his friends were doing something, but he hadn't been included. He didn't have anything to do, so he decided to talk to his youth pastor, Tom, a pretty nice guy. John thought Tom seemed to know a lot about God, and it didn't seem like the knowledge his parents spouted off about. Yet he had this annoying quality of asking questions that John did not want to answer because the questions forced him to think.

"Don't you think that seeing God as too busy brings Him down to your level?" Tom asked. "You know that God says His thoughts aren't like ours."

"I guess I never really thought of it that way." *Here we go again*, John thought, suddenly beginning to feel that he wanted out of this conversation. After all, his next date seemed more important than God at the present time. It made him uncomfortable to think that God actually thought about him.

But Tom wouldn't let it rest. "You know, John, God says His eyes are on those who hope in Him. That doesn't mean He is just watching until you slip up. Instead it means that you are the 'apple of His eye' and that He loves you so intensely He watches you to help you. It's a lot like the good basketball coach who watches his players to give them the instruction they need to be a winning team."

John gave that some thought, but he still wasn't convinced. He thought God was a lot like his earthly dad, who never seemed to think John did anything right.

Do the feelings John was experiencing seem familiar to you? It is vitally important that we understand just exactly how God sees us, rather than how we *think* He sees us, because these two things may not be the same.

What difference does it make? God is an important resource in your passage into adulthood. Let us give you an example. If something bad happens to you and you don't understand how much God loves you, you may assume that "fate" or "destiny" has it in for you. Also, when something bad happens, that is all there is. Nothing else. It's just bad. There is no real way to make sense of it, other than to say chance caused it to happen.

On the other hand, if you really believe God when He says He loves you and intends to give you hope and a future, then you may be better able to take such adversity in stride. Not only that, you can rest assured that God will do what He said He will do. Let's look at a few verses where God actually says how He feels about us:

> Look at the birds of the air, for they neither sow nor reap nor gather into barns; yet your heavenly Father feeds them. Are you not of more value than they? (Matt. 6:26)

If God cares for the birds of the air, will He care for your needs?
☑ yes   ☐ no

> For You formed my inward parts;
> You covered me in my mother's womb.
> I will praise You, for I am fearfully and wonderfully
>     made;
> Marvelous are Your works,
> And that my soul knows very well.
> My frame was not hidden from You,
> When I was made in secret,
> And skillfully wrought in the lowest parts of the earth.
> Your eyes saw my substance, being yet unformed.
> And in Your book they all were written,

> The days fashioned for me,
> When as yet there were none of them. (Ps. 139:13–16)

How does it feel to think that God knew all about you before you were even born?

☐ Uncomfortable          ☑ Comforting
☑ Good                   ☐ I can't imagine it!
☐ Scary                  ☐ I don't like it

But God demonstrates His own love toward us, in that while we were still sinners, Christ died for us. . . . For if when we were enemies we were reconciled to God through the death of His Son. . . . (Rom. 5:8, 10)

Would you die for an enemy?   ☐ yes  ☑ no
Are you worth dying for?   ☐ yes  ☑ no
What does God say? _Christ died for us_

---

> Bless the LORD, O my soul; . . .
> Who forgives all your iniquities,
> Who heals all your diseases, . . .
> Who satisfies your mouth with good things, . . .
> The LORD is merciful and gracious,
> Slow to anger, and abounding in mercy.
> He will not always strive with us,
> Nor will He keep His anger forever. (Ps. 103:2, 3, 5, 8, 9)

Love suffers long and is kind; love does not envy; love does not parade itself, is not puffed up; does not behave rudely, does not seek its own, is not provoked, thinks no evil; does not rejoice in iniquity, but rejoices in the truth; bears all things, believes all things, hopes all things, endures all things. Love never fails. (1 Cor. 13:4–8)

## Working It Out

Have your ideas changed about how God sees you? How would you summarize those ideas? Here are some of John's responses:

God sees me as someone *He loves enough to die for.*
God sees me as someone *He has set apart for a special purpose.*
God sees me as someone *He considers His child.*

OK, now it's your turn.

God sees me as someone who can be an enemy

God sees me as someone He wants to become his own

God sees me as someone He wants closer to him

God sees me as someone that tries to get closer but in return falls farther away

God sees me as someone He has to spread the word

# Chapter Eight

―――――――――――

# Putting It All Together

"**M**om, can I ask you a serious question?" John and his mother were sitting on the front porch of their home. The sun was just beginning to set above the houses across the street and a warm breeze was blowing. It was one of those perfect evenings when it's easy to feel peaceful and calm inside.

"Sure, John." His mom seemed a little startled by John's question. These talks hadn't occurred much lately because John had been so busy with school, sports, friends, his job, and other things, he wasn't around much.

"If you could live your life over again, what would you do differently when you were a teenager?" Just after he spoke, John realized it was an odd question to ask his mom.

She sighed deeply, sat back in her chair, and folded the corner of the page to mark her place in the book she was reading.

For almost an hour John and his mother talked about her childhood and the struggles she had growing up. John learned a lot that evening about his mom, but even more than that, his mom realized that her son was no longer the little boy she had held on her lap only a few years earlier. Little children almost never think about themselves in any really meaningful way.

They are too busy learning how to have fun, how to read, how to obey rules.

John's mom also recognized that John would be leaving home before long. Adolescence is the last phase of life in which you are dependent on your parents for many of the things necessary for living. As you grow and advance through this portion of your life, you become more and more independent from your family until, at the end, you are ready to live on your own.

Adolescence begins around junior high, when physical changes begin happening in your body. Those are really obvious because you and everyone else can clearly see them. What isn't so obvious is the psychological change going on inside you. That is just as important because your mind and emotions are doing the mental work to help you stand up on your own, without your parents making all the decisions for you. While John's mom had seen him maturing physically, she seemed a little startled when she realized he was developing psychologically as well.

Now your peers have started becoming more meaningful to you; in fact, sometimes what your peers think may be more important than what your family thinks. That is because you are now preparing to live in a society of your peers, completely independent from your parents.

Things like clothes, hairstyles, and outward appearance take up more of your time as you become more aware of how you look and act in public. How you act when you are around friends takes more thinking too. If you act totally childish people will say you are immature. So you have begun paying more attention to acting grown-up.

Little children often think their parents are the smartest people in the world. By now, you have probably begun to recognize that your parents are human and can make mistakes like everyone else. That also is an important part of this journey to adulthood, because realizing that parents aren't perfect allows you to see the world is a big place where people have all sorts of beliefs, many of which are different from your parents'. Until you recognize this, you are still dependent on your parents for everything you think.

This isn't to say your parents are wrong, stupid, or bad. They aren't. They once were adolescents, too, and can understand what you are going through. Because they gave birth to you and have watched you grow through every stage of your life, they probably know you better than anyone. Until the day you are completely ready to live independently it is important to live by their rules and values, which will assist you in the difficult process of becoming an adult.

In fact, you can still learn from them. John recognized that after the long discussion with his mom on the porch. Just because he had become more independent didn't mean his relationship with his mom was no longer necessary. Because of their time together, he learned that she had gone through some tough times, that she had struggled with her parents, and that she had a lot of questions about God as a teen.

There are three components to every person: physical, psychological, and most importantly, spiritual. King Solomon was a man who surely had every physical and psychological thing he wanted: clothes, money, large palaces, wisdom, many friends in high places, almost anything we can imagine. Yet that third component was missing, and he felt empty and hollow. He searched tirelessly for what life was all about, looking for that solid spiritual foundation.

At the end of his search he discovered something that can be helpful to you in your quest. He wrote, "Fear God and keep His commandments, for this is man's all" (Ecc. 12:13). Basically, he was saying that the entire meaning of life is allowing God to be in charge. To Solomon, a man who had everything, there was nothing more important than a relationship with God.

To do a really good job with this quest you have to be fully prepared physically, psychologically, and spiritually. Otherwise you run the risk of getting lost and never becoming a mature and complete adult. There are two final things you will need to understand to be ready spiritually to begin this quest.

First, you have to prepare by having a good goal in mind. Had Edmund Hillary not thought about his goal of reaching the top of Mount Everest, he would have given up before he ever got near the top. Like Hillary, you must have a goal for the quest you are now on.

The apostle Paul wrote:

> Do you not know that those who run in a race all run, but one receives the prize? Run in such a way that you may obtain it. And everyone who competes for the prize is temperate in all things. Now they do it to obtain a perishable crown, but we for an imperishable crown. Therefore I run thus: not with uncertainty. Thus I fight: not as one who beats the air. (1. Cor. 9:24–26)

Paul figured that the key to real growth and maturity was to develop a relationship with God that was solid enough to get him through the tough times. His goal was to put his relationship with God first, before anything else. That is why, when things got difficult, when he was beaten or put in prison, he was able to stay happy and content, even though the world seemed to be crashing in around him.

Like Paul, you will experience difficult times as you mature. Growing up can be very tough at times, and if you lose sight of what you are aiming for, you may begin to feel it is not worth the trouble. What exactly do you hope to accomplish at the end of your quest, when you are an adult? What are you aiming for? It is important to keep your eyes on the goal so, when the quest gets hard, you can still look ahead.

The second important part of preparation for the quest is having the right equipment. Edmund Hillary spent much time thinking about every piece of equipment he would need to scale the dangerous sides of Everest. Similarly, Paul told the Ephesians to "take up the whole armor of God, that you may be able to withstand in the evil day, and having done all, to stand" (Eph. 6:13). The best equipment for your quest will undoubtedly be the armor of God. It consists of:

1. The belt of truth (being honest)
2. The breastplate of righteousness (leading a clean life with God's help)
3. The shoes of the gospel of peace (finding God means knowing His Word)
4. The shield of faith (believing God will protect you)
5. The helmet of salvation (having relationship with God)
6. The sword of the spirit (allowing God's Spirit to guide our steps)

How about your own life? Do you have the right equipment for the difficult quest ahead? If you do, what condition is it in? Is it rusty due to lack of use, or is it in tip-top shape? Remember, good equipment can make or break any important quest.

Now let's put together these two parts of preparing for the quest, setting a goal and assembling your equipment. We'll help you sort out these steps by leading you through the following exercises.

## Working It Out

Spend a moment thinking about some of these changes that have taken place as you have moved out of childhood into adolescence. List a few of them below. John wrote:

1. *I pay more attention to the clothes I wear.*
2. *I'm spending more time with friends.*
3. *I've realized that my parents don't know everything.*
4. *I've noticed there are other ways of looking at the world than my parents' way.*

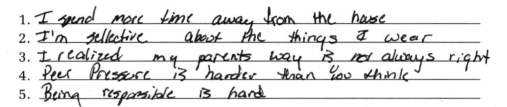

1. I spend more time away from the house
2. I'm sellective about the things I wear
3. I realized my parents way is not always right
4. Peer Pressure is harder than you think
5. Being responsible is hard

    The changes you just listed are important signs pointing to the fact that you, like John, have begun the process of maturing psychologically.

    Before you travel any farther in your quest, you need to decide what you want to accomplish. Do you wish to be able to live independently? Do you want more freedom? Do you need to be stronger, wiser, better able to handle difficult times? Think for a moment about what you hope to do between now and the time you reach adulthood. John listed these goals:

1. *I want to be mature enough to live on my own.*
2. *I want to be able to make good decisions without depending on my parents.*
3. *I want to be strong enough to not fall apart when things get tough.*

    Write your goal(s) here:

1. I want to make wise choices
2. Have freedom
3. I want to be emotionally strong

    Remember that goals can change. As you become more aware of what it means to be an adult, you may discover more things you need to work on, and these can then become part of your goals.

    Now check your equipment by completing the following inventory.

## 1. The belt of truth

Are you honest    ☐ All of the time     ☐ Some of the time
                   ☑ Most of the time     ☐ Rarely

What do you do when you know you are lying and need to admit to the truth? John wrote:

*I know I need to be more honest. I get myself in trouble sometimes by only telling part of the story and then I have to cover my tracks by making up more things to make the pieces fit together.*

How about you?

*I just say I was lying and tell the truth and go on.*

## 2. The breastplate of righteousness

Are you living your life by the values you know to be right?
☐ yes   ☑ no

Would God be pleased with your actions?   ☐ yes   ☑ no

Are there areas you need to work on?   ☑ yes   ☐ no

If so, are you ready for God to work with you on changing them?
☑ yes   ☐ no

What are some areas of your life where you need God's help to change? John said:

*I need to be able to stand up for what I know is right even when I'm afraid it might make me unpopular.*

Write your answer here:

*That I will not fall to peer pressure*

## 3. The shoes of the gospel

Do you read the Bible on a regular basis?   ☐ yes   ☑ no

Do you know the Bible well enough to use it when you make choices?  ☑ yes  ☐ no

How could you make the Bible more important to you and more helpful when you make important decisions about your quest? John's response was:

*I need to get up fifteen minutes earlier and read a little bit each day, maybe even memorizing some passages once in a while.*

What about you?

Read a little bit each day and become more familier with it.

### 4. The shield of faith

Do you believe God can and will protect you?  ☑ yes  ☐ no

If so, do you allow God to protect you, or do you usually try to control things yourself? John answered:

*My first response is usually to try it myself. I usually only bother God when things get really rough.*

When do you ask God for help?

I try to control it myself untill thing get really bad

### 5. The helmet of salvation:

Do you have a relationship with God?  ☐ yes  ☑ no

If so, have you paid much attention to it, or have you basically ignored God for a while? Do you talk with Him on a regular basis? John's response was:

*Sometimes I forget to pray. I probably could spend more time talking to God about everyday stuff like girls, school, and sports.*

What about you?

_I do not have a real strong relationship with God. I do for get to talk to him regularly_

## 6. The sword of the spirit

Do you allow God's Spirit to guide your conscience?   ☑ yes   ☐ no

When you make a mistake and realize it later, do you go back and make things right?   ☐ yes   ☑ no

When you know what you are doing is wrong, how do you respond? John wrote:

*There are times when I know I'm making the wrong decision, but it seems more fun than God's way. I usually do what I want and then feel guilty, but I don't pay much attention to my guilty feelings.*

What do you do?

_Sometimes I fix it but other times I just go on. Alot of times I will not do it but sometimes I will._

By the time John got to this point, he was thinking, *I've begun to realize that I never really had a goal in mind. I was just sort of getting older, hoping everything would fall into place.*

*I've also begun to realize that I've not paid a whole lot of attention to where God fits in with all this. I need to work on my relationship with God; that might make a difference in the way I deal with things in the future.*

# Chapter Nine

## What Good Is Looking Back?

**J**ohn couldn't figure it out. Why did Jennifer call him at home to make sure he was going to meet her at her locker? It didn't make sense. Of course he was going to be there. He was always there.

"Hi, John. I guess you're wondering why I called you last night, right?" Jennifer looked really uncomfortable. John was beginning to get a sinking feeling in his stomach. Suddenly he knew what was coming.

"Well, yeah. You know I always meet you here at your locker after first-hour class. What's going on?" John couldn't hide the anxiety in his voice.

"John, I want us to quit seeing each other for awhile. I just want to have a little more freedom and time to myself. It's nothing against you or anything. It's me. I just need some time to sort things out."

John knew this was the classic "Dear John" letter, except it was in verbal form. He was stunned. "I don't get it, Jennifer. What did I do? Why all of a sudden?"

"You didn't do anything, John. I just want to be free of any dating relationships for a while so I can spend more time with my friends."

That was little consolation to John. His mind was reeling. He really enjoyed going out with Jennifer and the special times they had together.

John simply turned and walked down the hall. He knew this was the end. He also wasn't about to fool himself into thinking she wanted to spend more time with her girlfriends. It was someone else. She was just trying to be nice.

It isn't easy to recover from a broken relationship because it's a real blow to your self-esteem. A situation like this can be quite influential in shaping how you think about yourself. John just might conclude that he really was as ugly and stupid as he feared and that no one could possibly like him.

In preparation for any journey, there is always a time for reflection and consideration of what one has done and how he or she has felt about these events. This type of reflection is not a selfish preoccupation. Jesus, in preparation for His ministry, went into the wilderness to consider what was ahead of Him.

In this chapter we'll ask you to spend some time reflecting on your life. Consider the people you have met, the activities and events you have participated in, that have somehow shaped you. Some of these events and people have been good for you, and some of these things have been very bad for you. As a matter of fact, some of these events and people have probably hurt you very deeply. These experiences have come together to shape you into who you are today.

Let us give you an example of the events and people who shaped one young man, the youngest kid in a very large family. His brothers resented him very much because he was the favorite of their father. Of course, he didn't do much to make himself likable. As a matter of fact, he once told his brothers that they would one day have to serve under his authority. This kid really knew how to win friends and influence people!

One day his brothers had had enough of his antics, and they decided to stage a murder—*his* murder. So when he brought them their lunch, they threw him into an empty well. His brothers soon decided they needed to get rid of the evidence, so they sold him to a traveling band of gypsies. He was soon sold again as a slave to a wealthy man of another country.

You can imagine some of the pain and rejection this young man felt. Perhaps feelings of pain and rejection are familiar to you. If so, you have just found an understanding friend in the biblical story of Joseph.

After a number of years had passed, Joseph met his brothers again in the rich man's house. They had come to get some food because there was a famine in their country and they were poor. Here they were, bowing to Joseph and asking for a handout!

Joseph had learned a great deal by this time. He knew what his brothers had done for evil, God had used for good. With that perspective, he was ready to move on and become the one who saved his brothers and their families, even though they had not treated him fairly.

Now it is your time to remember. To see your life from a broad perspective, use the next pages to list the things that have happened to you: the people, the places, the memories that are painful, the memories that bring a smile to your face. Remember as much as you can. It is important that you see just how far you have already come in your quest for truth. There will be events and experiences that you may want to pass over—a divorce, the death of a sibling, parent, or other relative, the loss of a pet. But don't leave these out.

## Working It Out

List five people who have been important to you in your life (parents, childhood friends, siblings, relatives, youth pastors, others). Also describe what made these people important to you. Here are three of the people John thought of:

1. *My youth pastor, Tom. He's important because he listens to me and helps me learn a lot about God.*
2. *Jim, my buddy when I was a kid. We did everything together, from playing soldiers to camping out. I could really trust him.*
3. *My grandfather. I really loved him. He would take me fishing and tell me stories of when he was a boy growing up in Ohio.*

Get the picture? Now it's your turn.

1. Elaine, My sister that has come Into my life and that I do love dearly

2. Kim, helped me sort through alot of my problems at Hus School.

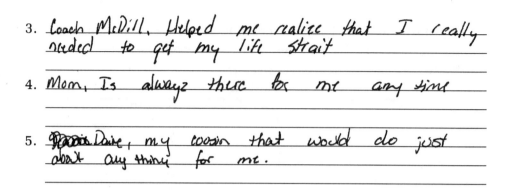

3. Coach McDill, Helped me realize that I really needed to get my life strait

4. Mom, Is always there for me any time

5. ~~Davie~~ Davie, my coosin that would do just about any thing for me.

Now, list three great things that have happened to you (for example, accomplishments you are proud of, events that made you feel really good, or other exciting events in your life). Here are two of the things John remembered:

1. *I really felt great when I made the basketball team after injuring myself in the off-season. I had really worked hard on strengthening my knee and a regular schedule of workouts.*
2. *Another really exciting time was when I got to meet Michael Jordan, the professional basketball player. I was so lucky to have him sign a basketball and give it to me. I still have it!*

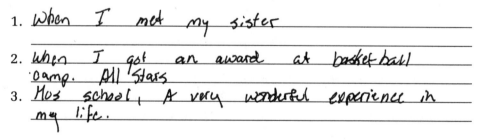

1. When I met my sister

2. when I got an award at basketball camp. All Stars

3. Mos school, A very wonderful experience in my life.

This next one will be a little tougher, but you can do it. We would like you to describe something bad that happened to you and ended up becoming something very important in your life. This is what we call a "Joseph" story. Here is John's:

One day in grade school I got in trouble and ended up in the principal's office. I was really in trouble, or so I thought. Instead of getting a swat, though, he talked to me and asked me how I was feeling. I said I didn't know, except I was mad about everything. I told him my grandpa had died about two weeks before. The principal told me he cared about me and he understood how hard it was to lose someone you love. He said it's pretty easy to be mad but you just don't know who to take it out on. I really needed that. That principal is someone I can now say is a good friend, and a really great supporter of almost anything I do. If he hadn't understood how I felt and listened to me, I probably would have been sent back to class only to get in trouble again later on.

Now write down your "Joseph" story:

When my mom told me and dad caught me smoking. I got in a lot of trouble but it made me realize what I was doing was wrong. It made me try to change my life around.

Reflect on what you have learned by looking back on your past. How has it felt? What was nice to see again? What still hurts? We'll get you started by showing you what John wrote.

## Travel Log

*Whenever I talked about the past with adults they always told me I was only dwelling on the past and needed to think about the future. That is what I have assumed all this time. When I finally took the time to look back, I realized there are some pretty cool things that have happened to me, and it really felt good to see I wasn't as much of a jerk as I was telling myself.*

*The problem is that when I looked back I also remembered the pain of losing my grandpa. That really hurt. It still hurts, but I guess that is OK. He was a great influence on me, and I can keep his memory alive by living as he taught me to live—honestly and caring about other people.*

*John*

Write your thoughts and feelings below.

## Date: _____

# Chapter Ten

Your Journey Up
to Now

You have just completed an inventory that helps you understand where you have come from—the important events, people, and decisions that have shaped your life. Seeing it in words, though, is often pretty lifeless and flat. So we would like you to make a map of your life.

  Imagine you were able to get above the "land" of your life and could see the path you have taken. What would that path look like? Would there be mountain ranges that represent the rough and hard times of your life? Would there be side roads that led nowhere, perhaps when you tried to start a new hobby or sport and didn't get anywhere? Have there been thunderstorms and rain clouds along the way that represent hard times that didn't last? Have you gotten lost as you have traveled through life? Maybe there are some really big holes you have fallen into, perhaps when someone who was really important to you died. What events, people, and decisions have made you who you are today?

  Here is what John's map looks like:

Notice that he included people on his map—his grandfather, his dad, and Jim, his friend from childhood. You probably can also see the rough times by his lightning bolts and thunderclouds. He also marked mountains and dead-end paths for relationships that led nowhere or were not good for him.

Now it's your turn. Use your imagination. This is for your eyes only. Draw a map of your life and the path you have taken to come to be the person you are today.

# PART TWO

## The Ascent

# Chapter Eleven

## Self-Doubt

*Sometimes I feel like a total failure. I look at my oldest sister, Debbie, and see how smart she is and how much my dad respects her, and I feel I can't measure up. So I get angry at him and we end up getting in another fight.*

*And I look at some of my friends who are so much cuter and more popular than I am and I wonder what makes me special. I'm reading all this stuff about preparing for adulthood and I think how much easier everyone else has it. It doesn't come naturally for me like it does for them. I just wish life were more fair! How am I ever going to be able to compete with those people who have it together when I feel like a total failure?*

*Beth*

Most long-distance trips seem to take forever. It's like when you go on vacation with your family: After what seems like ages, you look around and see that you're still just starting out. Sometimes minutes seem like hours and the miles seem to be creeping by at a snail's pace. Beth's quest was like that. She compared herself with others and got discouraged when she felt they were progressing faster than she was. She began to doubt her ability to finish the quest.

Beth felt she didn't measure up to her sisters and brothers, especially in her father's eyes. But instead of talking about it with him, she became angry and defensive. She stopped hearing what he had to say and relied too much on herself because she thought she would never earn his approval. She doubted herself and her ability to measure up to the others in the family.

Adventurers on this type of quest often make two mistakes: They rely too much on themselves, or they rely too much on others. The first mistake is dangerous because they don't get the information they need to finish the trip. The second is equally harmful, as we'll discuss in a moment.

The key to not making the mistake of relying too much on yourself is found in Proverbs 3:5–6: "Trust in the LORD with all your heart, / And lean not on your own understanding; / In all your ways acknowledge Him, / And He shall direct your paths." In other words, by trusting God's leadership and guidance (by asking for His help and by trusting the input given to you by others who have relied on God to complete their quest), you will avoid self-doubt because God will really be in charge of your adventure.

Relying too much on others can pose problems as well. Galatians 6:5 says, "each one shall bear his own load." When we doubt ourselves, we become afraid to make decisions we need to make. We tend to depend on others to make all the choices for us. That is an immature, childish way to deal with life's challenges.

Beth did this at times. She saw her friends as more popular and beautiful than she was and considered their opinions more valuable than her own. Since she didn't take a stand for what she wanted, she began to doubt whether or not she really could make good decisions.

A mature person makes good decisions based on solid information from Scripture, God's Word, and from trusted friends and family members. On the other hand, it is still your responsibility to actually *make* the decisions. If you are to be successful on your quest, you will have to learn how to collect as much information as possible from good sources and then make the best choice.

One final part of self-doubt is the fear of consequences. When you begin to take responsibility for yourself and your decisions, you run the risk of making the wrong choices once in a while. Sometimes people try to avoid the consequences of their decisions. Either they lie to cover their mistakes, or they play it safe and avoid trying new, adult behaviors that are important to growth. Beth played it safe by withdrawing from her family and not trying to compete and by allowing her friends to make all the important decisions.

The consequences of a poor decision help you make a different decision next time. Avoiding consequences is simply avoiding growth. While they sometimes are painful and unpleasant,they make you stronger, more mature, and better able to handle adult responsibility.

Since you will inevitably have some doubts about your ability to complete this quest, or about God's willingness to help you, it would be wise to think about how you respond to doubts.

## Working it Out

Why do you believe you sometimes doubt yourself? Beth answered:

*Because I rarely feel like I measure up to those around me. Everyone seems so much smarter, more popular, prettier, and more together than I do.*

_____

_____

_____

What sometimes happens that shakes up your self-confidence? For Beth it was:

*When my dad makes a comment about how smart my sister is, when guys seem to notice all my friends and not me, when I make a suggestion and everyone thinks it's dumb, and when I finally study really hard for a test and still make a C.*

What shakes your confidence? _____

_____

_____

List five times you've doubted yourself in the past:

1. _____
2. _____
3. _____

4. _____

5. _____

Think about these five instances. How did you handle the feelings of self-doubt? Did you:

- ☐ Quit
- ☐ Look to someone else to make the decision
- ☐ Get angry
- ☐ Act strong to cover up the fact that I had doubts
- ☐ Call myself stupid
- ☐ Blame someone else for making me have doubts
- ☐ Worry
- ☐ (Other) _____

In each of those situations, how could you have responded differently instead of doubting yourself?

- ☐ Looked to others for help
- ☐ Prayed about it
- ☐ Been more honest and dealt with the consequences
- ☐ Trusted myself more
- ☐ Allowed myself to make a mistake without calling myself stupid
- ☐ (Other) _____

Make a plan to deal differently with self-doubts when you have them in the future. Beth's plan went like this:

*I know I have a tendency to reject help from my family when I am doubting myself. In these situations I need to do just the opposite, and tell them I am feeling bad about what happened so they can know what I am feeling and give me their feedback. I need to express myself more with my friends. There are times I feel like I have something to say but hold back because I worry that it may be dumb. If they really are my friends, they will be able to handle it even if I make a dumb comment, so I will start giving my input into decisions instead of letting them make all of them.*

As you can see, Beth looked at why she responds as she does and tried to figure out ways to do just the opposite. Now it is your turn. Look over what you answered in the questions above. Then come up with ideas about how you can better handle times of self-doubt. Write your plan here:

_____

_____

_____

_____

_____

_____

_____

_____

# Chapter Twelve

---

# This Is Easier Than I Thought!

*I hate it when my mom is right! She was getting down on my choice of friends again. I started going out with Jake, a guy from the neighborhood, and my mother told me she knew him and he wasn't good for me. Of course, I got mad!*

*This time I thought I would act differently. Instead of yelling, I calmly stood up for myself. I told her I'm old enough now to start making decisions about who I go out with and I resent it when she tries to treat me like her baby daughter.*

*I thought I did the right thing and even my mom seemed impressed by the way I handled myself. But two weeks later I found out that Jake was cheating on me. Mom turned out to be right, and now I feel totally stupid. I feel even worse than I did before I tried standing up for myself.*

*What good is trying to do this stuff if it makes things worse?*
*Beth*

---

Sometimes when you learn something new, you can move too far in the opposite direction. After looking at self-doubt in the last chapter, you, too, might have felt more confident. *Perhaps this growth-and-truth stuff is easier than I'd imagined,* you may be thinking. You may even be wondering, *What's the big deal about adulthood anyway?*

Lots of kids we've worked with have had similar feelings early in the growth process. While it's OK to feel confident, especially if your confidence lies in God's ability to guide you, there is also a potential danger. That danger is pride.

Beth needed to recognize the difference between self-confidence and pride. Self-confidence comes from the feeling of a job well done. It is that inner glow that happens when you've completed a task you set out to do. It's the correct answer to self-doubt.

Pride, on the other hand, happens when you think too highly of yourself and your abilities. You believe you can do difficult things totally on your own, without help, God's or anyone else's. You set yourself up on a pedestal without the important input needed to help you successfully complete the quest. Proverbs 16:18 says, "Pride goes before destruction, / And a haughty spirit before a fall." You see, when you set yourself up like that, you're in a good position to fall.

Beth had become *overconfident,* or proud. She pushed too hard too soon, only to find that what she was learning about didn't just happen overnight. She needed to experiment a little and possibly fail once or twice before she got it just right. Instead, Beth jumped right in without asking anyone's input—and failed.

Here is a scale to help you understand the different between pride and self-confidence:

| **Self-Doubt** | **Self-Confidence** | **Pride** |
|---|---|---|
| "I can't do it." | "With help I can make it." | "I'll do just fine on my own." |

Pride is the opposite of self-doubt. If you are full of pride, you *do* believe in yourself, but you miss out on helpful and very valuable information from God and others who have been there and know what the road ahead is like. Self-confidence recognizes that you have the ability and *can* do it, but admits wisely that outside input is still quite important.

To venture into these mountains without input from those with experience would be foolish and would put your whole adventure in danger. Some, however, believe they can do it without any assistance whatsoever. These proud individuals are doomed to repeatedly get lost, fall into traps, pick poor traveling companions, and make other such mistakes.

Beth seemed to believe that maturity meant being completely on her own without accepting advice or help from others. Because of that, she tended to confuse pride with mature adulthood. Truly responsible adults admit they need help sometimes and ask for it. It's not immature or childlike to need help. In fact, asking for help when you need it is a very adult way to handle uncertainty.

Proud people are lonely people because they refuse to listen to others; eventually others stop trying to help. They are then left to themselves to make decisions that could be better handled with a little more information from others who really care and know the best routes to take.

To help you look at the pride in your own life and avoid the danger that can result, take some time to answer a few questions. Keep in mind the differences between self-confidence and pride. Sometimes people like Beth confuse the two and make serious mistakes.

## Working It Out

We've all had times when we thought too highly of ourselves, tried to do things without any help or outside information, and messed up because of it. This can happen with schoolwork, with difficult decisions we have to make, with our choice of friends, in sports, at our jobs—in fact, in almost any situation. Beth noted these times when pride caused her to make mistakes:

1. *My mom told me my old boyfriend, Jake, would use me, but I didn't listen and got real hurt when he cheated on me with someone else.*
2. *I didn't want to look stupid in geometry class, so I didn't ask an important question and totally messed up on the last test.*
3. *My dad tried to explain how to fix a flat tire, but I told him I already knew. So when I had a flat, I had to call him to come help me, and I felt really stupid.*

Now try some of your own:

1. _____
   _____
2. _____
   _____
3. _____
   _____

If you could do it again, how would you handle those times differently? Would you ask for help? Would you decide more carefully? Would you admit you didn't have the answers? Think about what you would need to do to make the situation better. Beth's answers were:

1. *I would have asked my mom why she thought Jake was bad for me.*
2. *I would have asked Mrs. Barnes the geometry question, even if it meant I might look stupid.*
3. *I would have admitted I didn't know how to fix a flat so I wouldn't have gotten stranded and had to call Dad.*

What would you have done differently?

1. _____
   _____
2. _____
   _____
3. _____
   _____

Recognizing that you *will* need help from others who have been where you're going, check the areas in which you will need help:

☐ Coping with peer pressure
☐ Keeping God part of my quest
☐ Having fun without getting into trouble
☐ Boyfriend or girlfriend relationships
☐ Dealing with stressful times
☐ Earning my parents' respect
☐ Standing up for my beliefs

- ☐ Worrying about future plans
- ☐ Developing more self-confidence
- ☐ Sex
- ☐ (Other) _____

Often pride creeps up on us, even before we are really aware of it. Who are some people you trust enough to tell you if you are endangering your quest?

**Friends**               **Adults**

1. _____    1. _____
2. _____    2. _____
3. _____    3. _____

This week make it a point to ask the people you have listed about areas of pride in your life.

After completing this section, you've probably realized some things about your own pride. Before you forget what you've learned about yourself, write it out in your Travel Log. We'll start you off with what Beth wrote in her log.

## Travel Log

*I guess I've realized some things about myself. I can't just change myself in one day. If I had talked with my mom about Jake instead of trying to convince her that I could handle myself without her advice, I wouldn't hurt so bad right now.*

*It's just not that easy to admit that Mom knows better than I do. I guess that's what pride is, thinking I'm right, even when others may know more than I do. I've got a lot to learn.*

*When I talked with Mom about all this, she didn't give me that old, "I-told-you-so" look. Instead, she told me that we all make mistakes and that she still loves me, even if I'm not perfect. Maybe she is one of the people I need to talk to this week about pride.*

*Beth*

Now write out what you're thinking, feeling, and learning.

**Date:** _____

_____

_____

_____

_____

_____

_____

_____

_____

_____

_____

_____

_____

_____

_____

_____

_____

_____

_____

_____

_____

_____

_____

_____

_____

_____

_____

_____

_____

_____

_____

_____

_____

_____

_____

# Chapter Thirteen

## Who's Coming with Me?

One day John and his friend Jason were standing outside their next class. It was their usual ritual. Neither one of them was anxious to go into this one—chemistry.

You might remember Jason, the free-wheeling kid who pressured John to drink a beer. The fact that he would often get into trouble with the law and teachers only made him more interesting. John found, though, that the more he was around Jason the more he was doing and saying things he wouldn't normally do or say.

John's friend, Joy, had just come to her locker to pick up some books for her next class. Before John could say "Hi," Jason spoke up.

"Hey, Joy, where did you get that dress, K-Mart?" That drew a round of chuckles from Jason's friends, standing nearby.

Joy was obviously embarrassed by the remark, but she didn't say anything. Unfortunately, her locker was right in front of their classroom door.

"You know, Joy, there's more to life than school. Of course, when you don't get asked out, there isn't much else to do, right?"

John didn't know what to say. It suddenly felt like someone had turned the school into a sauna. He didn't want to lose Jason's friendship, but he also didn't like Jason's cruel remarks. John did the worst possible thing; he didn't say anything.

Joy turned around and faced her accusers. "If I were you, Jason, I wouldn't give too many people a piece of your mind. You don't have too much to spare!" Her eyes flashed. She looked squarely at John, then turned and walked down the hall. John felt like he was an inch tall. He had abandoned a friend when she needed him most. He really was a jerk. He knew he might as well have joined in and laughed right along with Jason's other friends. His silence had been a quiet form of encouragement. John needed to choose better traveling companions.

What would one of your first tasks be on a mountain-climbing trip? To choose your traveling companions. Who will you take on this grueling adventure? Not just anyone, but someone you can trust. Who you choose will often influence how you deal with the obstacles ahead.

Some traveling companions may look pretty good at first, as Jason did, but these "friends" may turn out to be the worst ones. You cannot underestimate the degree of influence your traveling companions can have on you, even if you're not aware of it, until you get some honest feedback from someone outside your circle of friends.

The hardest thing to remember is that you have the right to pick and choose who you will allow to come along with you on this adventure. Many teens feel that if someone likes them, they *have* to return those feelings. These people may not be wise traveling companions.

Take a moment and describe three of your best friends. What are they like? Don't sugarcoat it. Be totally honest. Now think about what the Bible has to say about the influence of your friends:

Do not be deceived: "Evil company corrupts good habits." (1 Cor. 15:33)

My son, do not walk in the way with them, / Keep your foot from their path. (Prov. 1:15)

Do not enter the path of the wicked, / And do not walk in the way of evil. (Prov. 4:14)

You shall not follow a crowd to do evil; nor shall you testify in a dispute so as to turn aside after many to pervert justice. (Exod. 23:2)

The writers of the Bible seem convinced that the people you choose to hang out with are important to you. What people would you choose as your traveling companions? People who only tell you what you want to hear, whether or not it is right? These people are the "yes men." They are so desperate to have friends they wouldn't disagree if their lives depended on it. This type of person is a hazard to your quest because he or she is not willing to give an alternative opinion that could help you in the long run.

Or would you choose those who allow you to make all the choices for them? If you ask these people what they want to do, they will say, "Oh, whatever you want is fine." Or are you the kind who wants someone to make all the choices for you? Or would you choose someone with values like yours? Do you want a traveling companion who has a strong sense of values and can help you choose the best path? (Or do you want someone who takes a "live-and-let-live" attitude toward life?)

Take time now to consider the kind of traveling companion you desire.

## Working It Out

The five most important characteristics of a traveling companion are (John listed *trustworthy, helpful, loyal, open-minded*):

1. _____
2. _____
3. _____
4. _____
5. _____

The five most important characteristics I need to avoid in a traveling companion are (John wrote, *People who get in trouble or abuse drugs and alcohol. People who talk too much. People who are only out for themselves*):

1. _____
2. _____
3. _____
4. _____
5. _____

The five most dominant characteristics of my current traveling companions through life are (John wrote, *Some often get in trouble, some are straight, some attend church, some are sexually active, some abuse drugs or alcohol.*):

1. _____
2. _____
3. _____
4. _____
5. _____

Name one traveling companion who was a poor choice. Tell why it was a bad choice (John admitted, *Jason led me down the path of trouble with teachers. I had more important things to do than in-school suspension. He seemed to have so much fun, but I found out it was just a big show. Behind it was someone who was really miserable. I didn't need to be around that. I've got enough troubles of my own!*):

1. _____
2. _____
3. _____
4. _____
5. _____

What kind of values will you look for in a traveling companion?

☐ Honest
☐ Trustworthy
☐ Good sense of humor
☐ Open-minded
☐ Intelligent
☐ Independent

☐ Isn't an alcoholic
☐ Doesn't get into trouble
☐ Loyal friend
☐ Has dreams for the future
☐ Doesn't spread vicious rumors
   about others

- ☐ Not afraid to stand up for what is right
- ☐ Respect for my values
- ☐ Values and respects people
- ☐ Willing to help others
- ☐ Believes in God
- ☐ Keeps promises
- ☐ Willing to admit mistakes
- ☐ Respects my decisions (won't try to talk me into getting into trouble)
- ☐ Doesn't do drugs
- ☐ Doesn't always have to be "right"
- ☐ Doesn't boast or brag about himself or herself
- ☐ Humble about abilities
- ☐ Can keep confidential information
- ☐ Isn't "easy" sexually
- ☐ Can take disagreement with his or her point of view
- ☐ (Other) _____

Who will go with me on my quest?

- ☐ Parents
- ☐ Counselors
- ☐ Brothers and sisters
- ☐ Coaches
- ☐ Youth pastor
- ☐ Relatives
- ☐ Friends
- ☐ Girlfriend/boyfriend
- ☐ Teachers
- ☐ An adult I trust (Whom? ____)
- ☐ (Other) _____

Look at the list above and put a plus sign (+) after the ones who will push you to be your best and a minus sign (-) after the ones who might have a negative influence on you. Make a separate list of the people who will have a positive influence on you and consider ways you can spend more time with them.

# Chapter Fourteen

---

# Sidetracks and Obstacles

*Sometimes I wonder where my life is headed. My mom seems to know where her life is going. She often talks of how God is her guide and she is following Him. But she's older and isn't faced with the same decisions I am. There seem to be so many things I want. I sometimes think fun with friends is the most important thing. Other times I think I should do better in school so I can go to college like everyone else in my family. Once in a while I think I should follow God, but other times I wonder if all that God stuff is really true. There's so much out there, but not enough time to try it all. I wish I could figure out what really matters.*

*Beth*

It's very common to wonder just where your life is headed. It's part of the preparation for becoming an adult. Like Beth, you may be asking deep questions such as, "Where is my life headed?" and "Why do I exist?" and "What is the meaning behind my life?"

Many paths twist and wind through the mountains of adolescence, all of them calling you to follow. You have to choose carefully which one you will follow or you will never reach your goal of becoming an adult. If you don't travel the right path, you run the risk of constantly exploring the many sidetracks that lead away from the narrow and sometimes hazardous road that leads directly to truth and maturity. And even if you do choose the right path, you may encounter many obstacles to growth that can cover the main route and make it difficult to see the road clearly.

For example, as you learned from watching Beth, pride and self-doubt can become obstacles that make it confusing to find and follow the path to maturity. Angry feelings can also block the road to growth. They keep you focused on the persons or events that made you angry and lead you away from the narrow, poorly marked trail. Hurt feelings can hinder growth, too, because people in pain often begin to think growth is too difficult.

There will be times that, like Beth and John, you find these obstacles blocking the path to adulthood. Other times, you will be tempted to walk down some dangerous sidetracks and risk getting lost. Lots of side trails seem more exciting and offer more adventure and fun than the path you've chosen. They are also a lot easier to follow because so many others are traveling them and seeming to have a great time. But Solomon wrote this about following such trails: "There is a way that seems right to a man, / But its end is the way of death" (Prov. 14:12).

Sometimes you may be tempted to follow a friend down one of these sidetracks. That's what happened when Beth's friend Jeanne talked her into going out one night with two guys who had pretty bad reputations. Beth believed Jeanne when she said the guys weren't really as bad as everyone said, so she went along. Because the guys tried to pressure the girls into sex, the date was a disaster and Beth was mad. Jeanne later apologized and admitted that she really hadn't known them that well.

Some friends are aware that they are lost and they may even feel bad about it. Or they may be angry about life, feeling the main path is too difficult or boring, so they choose another way. Whatever their feelings are about the side trail they've chosen, they don't want to be alone on it, so they try to talk others into joining them. Be careful about following these individuals. It is only after you realize how far from the main path they have led you that you understand the danger of following them.

Not all side trails involve major mistakes like sex, drugs, or alcohol. Sometimes they can be as simple as not dealing with problems. For example, when Beth was compared to her siblings, she thought others were being unfair to her and she became angry. She would go to her room, close the door, and avoid talking to her family for the next week or so. Since Beth rarely spoke her mind and talked about what was bothering her, things never got worked out and she ended up feeling as if no one cared about her side of things. Walking away only caused worse feelings of self-doubt and inferiority, a path that led away from maturity.

Inside all of us is the "fight-or-flight" response to threats. When problems occur, like family problems, girlfriend or boyfriend problems, or unhappiness, guilt, anger, and worry, you react in one of two ways. You either stand and work out the situation (fight) or you run away from it (flight). When you run from problems, you don't always take the time to consider the path you are taking. Only later do you realize the mistake, often after it is too late to easily get back to where you started.

Working out problems means thinking about them, coming to some plan of action that could help make things better, trying the plan, and coming up with a new one if the first one doesn't work. This may seem hard, but it is much better than trying to find your way back to the main trail after you have gotten lost running down a sidetrack. We'll walk you through the process in the following exercises.

## Working It Out

Use this outline to develop your own plan for resolving conflict.

**The problem:**

I get angry at my dad when he compares me to my siblings.

**What can I do?**
(List my alternatives.)

1. Talk to him about it
2. Run away from home
3. Yell and scream at him

**Plan**
(Choose the best alternative.)

I'll talk to Dad about my angry feelings.

**Act**
(Try out the plan I've chosen.)

Plan the best time and place to talk with dad, then do it.

**Evaluate**
Did my chosen plan work?

☐ yes  ☐ no

**I would do these things the same next time:**

1. Pick a quiet place.

2. Talk to Dad when he is in a good mood.

3. Plan out exactly what I wish to say.

**I would do these things differently:**

1. Make sure I'm not still feeling mad.

2. Not have a lot of homework to do.

3. Thank Dad for listening and caring.

You can practice this exercise in the space below. Think of a specific problem you need to work out, then plug in the steps. Here goes:

**The problem:** _____

**What can I do?**
(List my alternatives.)

1. _____
2. _____
3. _____

**Plan**
(Choose the best alternative.)

_____
_____

**Act**
(Try out the plan I choose.)

Best time _____
Best place _____

**Evaluate**
Did my chosen plan work?

☐ yes   ☐ no

**I would do these things the same next time:**

1. _____
2. _____
3. _____

**I would do these things differently:**

1. _____
2. _____
3. _____

It may take some getting used to, but dealing with problems is a much more mature way of handling them than running from them. Remember that anything that is worthwhile takes time and energy.

If you find yourself on a sidetrack, don't get too discouraged. God has been through this with lots of people; He can help you find your way back. David understood this when he said, "Show me Your ways, O LORD;/ Teach me Your paths" (Ps. 25:4).

The following questions will help you consider the many paths and obstacles you will encounter on your quest.

What is the path you believe you should be on? Beth wrote:

*Even though I don't act like it, sometimes I know I should be on the straight and narrow path that leads to maturity and truth. It is the path of following God.*

How about you?

_____

_____

Check the difficulties you might encounter on this path:

☐ Friends making fun of me
☐ Parents not trusting me
☐ Getting bored
☐ Immature friends
☐ Wanting more excitement
☐ Competition with brothers and sisters

☐ Getting discouraged when maturity takes too long
☐ Not knowing which way to go sometimes
☐ Peer pressure to go another way
☐ Difficulty trusting God
☐ (Other) _____

Check the wrong paths you have taken or might mistakenly take:

☐ Drugs
☐ Anger
☐ Alcohol
☐ Self-injury
☐ Sex

☐ Running away
☐ Thrill-seeking behavior
☐ Eating disorders
☐ Bitterness
☐ (Other) _____

Some people who might help me find the right path are:

☐ My pastor or youth leader
☐ My parents
☐ Friends who are a positive influence

☐ Relatives I trust
☐ Other Christians
☐ (Other) _____

Some people who might lead me astray are:

☐ Friends with authority problems
☐ People who pressure or try to control me

☐ Dishonest friends
☐ Drinking or drug-using buddies
☐ (Other) _____

Think about what might assist you in more wisely walking the path you know you wish to be on. List a few ideas.

_____

_____

# Chapter Fifteen

## The Pit

*I'm really stuck. My parents don't believe anything I say anymore, and I'm grounded for two weeks on top of it. I guess it started when I came home after curfew. Jennifer and I had gotten back together and we were making out, and I lost track of time. It was only a half-hour, but my parents made a pretty big deal of it. Naturally I couldn't tell them the truth. They seemed to know the reasons I gave them weren't true, but they let me go with a warning.*

*The next day a few of my friends told me some of the excuses they use on their parents when they come home late. I got some pretty good ideas from them. But they didn't tell me that most of the time those excuses don't work.*

*About a week had gone by and the same thing happened. This time I was about forty-five minutes late. I tried a couple of my friends' excuses and my parents started figuring out that I was lying. Things really heated up until we were in a big fight, and now I'm grounded for two weeks. All my plans have to be canceled, including the trip to the lake with some of my buddies. And my par-*

*ents will never trust me again because they know I lied. I feel really bad, like there's no way out.*

*John*

Picture yourself on the trail. The road has been rocky and tough but you've avoided problems fairly well recently and you're feeling pretty confident. Telling yourself it's time to rest, you decide to seek refuge in a cave that looks cool and inviting. You step inside, feeling your way in the darkness. Before you realize what's happened, you've fallen into a deep, muddy pit.

Several others are down there, too, stuck in the muck. Their stories sound much like your own. They have tried frantically to escape from the pit, but the sides are too slick. Now they sit hopelessly at the bottom, believing escape is impossible.

You have had other discouragements like this on your quest. Throughout this adventure there were trials and difficulties that at first seemed totally impossible. Each time you looked to God and His Word for leadership and guidance and found that things were not as bad as they seemed. You recall Jesus' words in Luke 18:27, "The things which are impossible with men are possible with God."

At this point you are faced with a choice. On the one hand, you can join the others in believing you will never escape from the pit. Or you can admit you've made a mistake and turn to God for a creative solution to a problem that would be impossible for you to handle alone.

In real-life terms, a pit is a situation that feels impossible. For instance, you might believe you can never do well in school, or you can never get along with your parents, or never stop drinking, drugging, and partying.

John fell into his pit by repeatedly breaking his curfew and then lying about why it happened. In addition to breaking the rules, he had lost his parents' trust, something that was important to him. He knew if they didn't trust him, they would have difficulty allowing him the freedom he really desired. The situation seemed impossible.

Everyone has fallen into a pit at one time or another. That's part of the quest. But pits don't have to mean failure. You only fail when you stop turning to God, an expert at delivering people from hopeless situations.

Jonah knew this; that's why he said, "I went down to the moorings of the mountains;/The earth with its bars closed behind me forever;/Yet You have brought up my life from the pit,/O LORD, my God" (Jonah 2:6).

The difference between those who climb out of the pit and those who give up is the recognition that with God, anything is possible.

Make some decisions about what to do when you feel stuck in hopeless or seemingly impossible situations. Don't spend too long at the bottom of these pits because eventually you will become like the others down there who have given up.

## Working It Out

Some pits into which I have fallen in the past are:

☐ Addictions
☐ Persistent worry
☐ School problems
☐ Depression

☐ Family conflicts
☐ Thinking I was a failure
☐ Anorexia/bulimia
☐ (Other) _____

In these pits, what have others told you that discouraged you or made it worse?

☐ It's impossible.
☐ You're a failure.
☐ It's not worth it.
☐ Why bother trying?

☐ Just don't worry about it.
☐ Forget about it; it will go away.
☐ That's nothing compared with my situation.
☐ (Other) _____

I have felt _____ (sad, angry, hopeless, etc.) in the past when I've stayed in one of these pits a long time because I:

☐ Thought it was impossible
☐ Gave up
☐ Tried to make the best of a bad situation
☐ Didn't know what to do
☐ Didn't realize I was stuck

☐ Thought it was normal
☐ Wanted others to think I had it together
☐ Couldn't admit I was stuck
☐ Was afraid to try and fail
☐ (Other) _____

In the future when I get stuck in these pits, I can:

☐ Pray
☐ Ask for help from others I
   trust
☐ Talk to someone about it

☐ Look for other ways out
☐ Admit I'm stuck and can't get
   out
☐ (Other) _____

If you are to become a solid adult, you must be able to recognize and deal with situations that seem hopeless. The moment you quit is the exact time you stop maturing.

# Chapter Sixteen

## Are We Having Fun Yet?

*It's tough putting all this quest stuff into practice. Oh, it sounds good enough when you read about it, but it's totally different when you actually try to do it. Sometimes I just have to ask, Are we having fun yet?*

*I've really tried to be more honest with others about who I am inside, but that creates problems sometimes, like when friends think I'm strange for not being fake and pretending everything is OK when it's not. Or when I try to talk about my feelings and my sister says she went through the same thing when she was my age, and then acts like she's so much older and more mature.*

*Besides that, there's just a lot to remember. And I get nervous, worrying if I don't get it right, I'll mess things up totally. This stuff all pays off in adulthood, they say. But that is a long way in the future.*

*In the meantime growing up seems like so much hard work*

*that I sometimes just want to go back to being a kid. It sure was easier back then. I didn't have to think so much. I feel exhausted and worn down. I'm not sure if I can handle all this, and I'm wondering if it's really worth it.*

*Beth*

Beth was feeling so exhausted and worn down by this adventure, it didn't seem exciting any longer. All these changes can be tiring and leave a person feeling run down. That's why fatigue is a normal part of adolescence.

There are two types of fatigue. The first kind is a breathless feeling that comes from physical exertion. Your lungs heave and gasp for air, and you have to stop for a while. The second kind is an aching deep within the muscles; it even seems to affect your mind. While the first type disappears as soon as you catch your breath, the second kind often sticks around for awhile.

Both types of fatigue are present on this adventure, but the psychological and emotional fatigue is more common than the physical type. Sometimes this growing-up stuff can leave you feeling completely worn down. You look at how much still lies ahead of you and you begin to feel discouraged, maybe even hopeless. This is a lot like the discouragement Beth felt when she wrote that it was easier being a kid. It caused her to wonder if growing up was really worth the work it took.

Because of her frustration, Beth thought about giving up and quitting. She felt hopeless and helpless. Instead of being excited about how far she had traveled, she could only feel overwhelmed by how far she still had to go.

When they feel frustrated, some teens try to push themselves harder to complete the growth process even faster, thinking it's taking too long. But rushing maturity only makes the process harder, especially when you're already feeling exhausted. Maturity, when done correctly, takes time.

So you are now faced with yet another choice. Should you quit and turn back, or press on, despite your fatigue? If you quit or turn back, all the progress you have made will be lost. Those who fail to continue will never reach true maturity. They will be kids in adult bodies, pretending to be grown.

On the other hand, you could decide to continue forward. Because of your fatigue, this will be difficult, but in the long run it will be well worth the effort. Perhaps it will help to think of the fatigue you feel as a sign that you are becoming more mature and getting ready to handle the challenges of the future.

And in case you've forgotten, there is an important resource at your disposal. God has more than enough strength to help you keep moving. Paul knew when he was exhausted and weak, God was able to do His best work in him. Paul wrote, "And He said to me, 'My grace is sufficient for you, for My strength is made perfect in weakness'" (2 Cor. 12:9).

Isaiah took it a step further, and wrote about the fatigue that teens feel:

> He gives power to the weak, and to those who have no might He increases strength. Even the youths shall faint and be weary, and the young men shall utterly fall, but those who wait on the LORD shall renew their strength; they shall mount up with wings like eagles, they shall run and not be weary, they shall walk and not faint. (Isa. 40:29–31)

This is the source of refreshment, even for those who have experienced the deepest, most despairing fatigue. God has promised not to abandon you or let you down, especially when you are exhausted. In fact, God's help is strongest when you are at your weakest because you are forced to rely on His strength and power more than your own.

Remember, though, it's pretty hard to experience God's rest if you're too proud to admit you're tired! Watch out for pride. It can keep you from taking advantage of what God offers you.

## Working It Out

These are some times when I have felt emotional fatigue:

- ☐ When I've argued with my parents
- ☐ When I've broken up with my girlfriend or boyfriend
- ☐ When school got really difficult
- ☐ When I was embarrassed in front of people I was trying to impress
- ☐ When I've been pressured by others to do things I didn't want to do
- ☐ When I felt that life was just too hard
- ☐ When I thought no one understood me or my problems
- ☐ When I failed at an important task
- ☐ (Other) _____

When you felt fatigued, what did you do?

☐ I quit
☐ I pushed myself harder until I felt even worse
☐ I started to put myself down for not being stronger
☐ I didn't do anything because I believed things were impossible
☐ I acted angry, and hurt those around me
☐ (Other) _____

When I feel exhausted and hopeless in the future, instead of simply giving up I could:

☐ Ask God for help
☐ Take some time to rest
☐ Live one day at a time instead of worrying about the future
☐ Talk to someone I think might understand
☐ Do something I enjoy to reward myself for working so hard
☐ Tell myself that being tired is a natural part of growing up
☐ (Other) _____

Who can you turn to for help when you feel like quitting? (List several people who would understand the kind of fatigue you are experiencing.)

1. _____
2. _____
3. _____
4. _____

It's a pretty exhausting world we live in. Fortunately, God's power is strongest in our lives when we are at the end of our own strength.

# Chapter
# Seventeen

# A Time to Reflect

Counselors at a camp on Lake Huron used to take groups of campers on island outings in a thirty-four-foot canoe that was a replica of the canoes used
to transport goods in the late 1800s. When the group reached an island, the
counselors would ask one of the older campers to "solo" there. The camper
was to take a tarp, a Bible, string, his journal, and lots of water, and find a
solitary place on the island to set up a little camp. He would spend the afternoon and night alone on the island, and the next morning the group would
return to pick him up. The campers had been prepared for such adventures;
that was part of the camp program.

When the solo camper rejoined the group, he would talk about what
he had experienced, what he had thought about, what had happened.

Even though the camp program had prepared the campers for this
experience, the counselors came to expect an argument when it was time to
send one of them off on his solo outing. The teenagers complained that they
didn't know what to do with themselves. For most of their lives they had
been entertained and amused by others. They had spent very little time

alone. In spite of this, the counselors would prevail and the camper would trudge off on his solo adventure.

The thoughts the campers shared when the counselors came to get them the next morning were always worth the arguments and coaxing that had preceded the assignment. For example, one young man came back from his solo and said, "I have never had to just sit and think. It was boring at first. Then I began thinking about our trip so far and how far we have come. We were really terrible at paddling the canoe at first. We were lucky we didn't go in circles all the time! Now we move across the water like ice on a mirror. I thought about the friends I have made. I wrote down everything we've done on our entire trip so far. It was neat to see all that we have done together."

He was proud of what he had done on his solo adventure. In a quiet and solitary place, he had taken time to reflect on his trip, and the good feelings that resulted from that reflection were invigorating. That is your job now, to take time out to reflect on where you've been and where you are going.

Jesus knew the value of reflection and time alone to order his priorities and gather strength to continue his daily routine. He also spent time alone in prayer. Notice these verses:

> Now in the morning, having risen a long while before daylight, He went out and departed to a solitary place; and there He prayed. (Mark 1:35)

> So He Himself often withdrew into the wilderness and prayed. (Luke 5:16)

Some people, like the campers, think there's something frightening about solitude and reflection. But Jesus knew—and you will learn as you experience reflective solitude—that times of reflection are valuable, not frightening. They help us barricade ourselves away from the hustle and bustle of the world and focus on our lives and where we are heading.

In your private time, consider what new things you have learned about yourself on your quest. What surprises did you find? What were some things you found that you didn't like? As you begin, consider these words about the wisdom of reflecting from the Book of Psalms:

> I remember the days of old;
> I meditate on all Your works;
> I muse on the work of Your hands. (Ps. 143:5)

When I consider Your heavens, the work of Your fingers,
The moon and the stars, which You have ordained,
What is man that You are mindful of him,
And the son of man that You visit him? (Ps. 8:3–4)

We would like to mention one other benefit of reflective time. When you reflect on your life, you will also see just how faithful God has been through your quest to protect you, care for you, comfort you, and carry you when you were too weak to go on. Sometimes it's pretty hard to see while it's happening. You have to step off the trail for a moment, find a quiet place, and look back. That is what reflection does for us, just like it did for David when he penned those psalms.

## Working It Out

List three things you have learned about yourself that you didn't know before you started the quest. We'll get you started by sharing what Beth wrote:

1. *I found that I carry other people's burdens more for myself than for them. I don't like to see people unhappy.*
2. *Sometimes I get myself in trouble by thinking that one success is proof that everything will be fine. That sets me up for disappointment.*
3. *I don't handle loss well. I choose a lot of unhealthy ways to comfort myself—eating, getting mad at others, being sarcastic, shopping.*

Now it's your turn:

1. _____
2. _____
3. _____

What are the areas that cause you to struggle the most?

☐ Self-doubt      ☐ Doubting God's goodness
☐ Choosing healthy friends      ☐ Carrying others' burdens
☐ Getting sidetracked      ☐ Carrying grudges
☐ Understanding how God sees me      ☐ Taking time to reflect

☐ Fatigue
☐ Comforting myself in unhealthy ways

☐ Pride
☐ Coping with mistakes and
   "falling down"

When a person takes time to reflect on his or her life and values, he or she might not like what is found. Is that what happened to you?
☐ yes  ☐ no

If that happened to you, what are some things you found out about yourself that you didn't like? Here's what Beth wrote:

*I am beginning to see my tendency to do things that are just the opposite of what people tell me, just to prove that I can do what I want. But sometimes I choose things that really don't help me much. I don't like that.*

Now it's your turn:

_____

_____

_____

_____

So, now that you have spent some time thinking about the things you have learned so far, what are you going to do about it? What areas are you going to work on? Here's what Beth wrote:

1. *I need to work on choosing healthier friends because I want to, not just because my parents approve.*
2. *I also need to find better ways to deal with the pain I feel over losing someone. It's not that I'm not supposed to feel bad. But I need to find healthier ways to comfort myself.*

Now it's your turn:

1. _____
2. _____
3. _____

# Chapter Eighteen

## There's a Hole in My Heart

"Dad, have you ever had anything happen to you that makes you feel like someone has ripped a hole in your heart?"

John was struggling to hold back the tears. He had just found out that a really good friend had almost been killed by a drunk driver. Jack was in a coma, and his doctors had said they really didn't expect him to come out of it.

John's dad thought a minute. "Yes, John, I have. When I was in high school a friend of mine worked on a golf course with me. Terry was his name. He and I had great times together while we worked on the greens. Well, one night he was out with a mutual friend of ours and they were drinking. Terry never did drive very carefully, and this night was no exception. They missed a turn in the road and took out three telephone poles. He was killed instantly."

His dad stopped, faltering a moment. It was obvious a lot of feelings were still left in that emotional wound. John had never seen his dad that way before.

Finally his dad continued, "When I first heard the news, I just denied that it was true. I couldn't believe it. I had just seen Terry that afternoon. He was fine. I never dreamed he would be stupid enough to drink and drive. Afterward, I got really mad at anything I could get mad at—the doctors for not saving Terry, his parents for not grounding him so he couldn't have gone out, the store that sold him the alcohol. I even got mad at myself for not being there to convince him not to drink and drive. Finally, though, I got to the point where I could go to his grave and say good-bye. It was really hard. He was a good friend."

John's dad sighed as he recalled the final good-bye.

John was stunned. His dad had felt all the things he was feeling about Jack. It was comforting to know his dad could understand.

"Dad, I just found out Jack was in an accident, too."

John's dad pulled his chair closer to his son.

"He was hit by a drunk driver, Dad, and he's in a coma." John started crying uncontrollably. The sobs burst out of him like a flood. It hurt so bad to think his friend was in a hospital and he couldn't do anything about it. John's dad put his arm around him and let him cry. "John, I am so sorry about your friend. I just can't tell you how sorry I am."

Sooner or later, we all experience loss in our lives. These casualties may not necessarily be people. They can be lost relationships or not making the cheerleading squad or an athletic team. Whatever the casualty, you are likely to feel many of the same emotions John expressed, with varying intensity depending on the loss.

The loss of a friend or loved one is probably the most painful, whether it is through death or a broken relationship. The pain is immense, and it seems you will never get over it. It tends to throw you into a tailspin, sometimes making you behave in ways you never thought possible.

Your first response to this kind of loss is probably denial. You say to yourself, *This can't be happening. It's all a dream, and when I wake up it will all be back to normal.* But of course, it's not a dream; that person is gone from your life. You are faced with a decision about how you will comfort yourself. You may say inwardly, *Where can I turn for some pain relief?*

When you were faced with a loss, no matter how great or small, how did you cope? Some ways of dealing with grief and loss are healthy, and some are not. For example, some teens have an overwhelming desire to pull away from everyone and try to comfort themselves. It seems safer that way. After being hurt so badly, grieving teens often opt not to get involved with people because they don't want to risk another lost relationship.

Other teens are willing to talk and cry openly; they give themselves permission to feel their feelings, whatever they are. But it's pretty hard to accomplish this because most people probably won't understand openly expressed emotions. They believe feelings are to be expressed in private and not in public, and they are uncomfortable with others' feelings of loss.

Finally, some teens deal with loss through ways that allow them to escape reality. These ways include addictive behaviors such as compulsive overeating and other eating disorders such as anorexia and bulimia, alcohol and drug abuse, codependency (an addiction to people), and other compulsive behaviors.

You are probably wondering what these addictive behaviors have to do with comforting oneself. What they offer is an escape from reality. For example, the person who abuses alcohol is seeking, for a brief moment, to make believe the loss hasn't really happened. And if it didn't happen, he or she doesn't have to feel any pain.

The pain of loss and the need for comfort was not a foreign idea to Jesus. The Bible highlights a variety of times when Jesus experienced the sting of loss—not only the loss of His friend Lazarus, but also the loss of relationships when His disciples abandoned Him. Here are a few verses to remind you of the comfort God offers those who face the pain of loss.

> Let, I pray, Your merciful kindness be for my comfort,
> According to Your word to Your servant. (Ps. 119:76)

> As one whom his mother comforts, so I will comfort you; and you shall be comforted in Jerusalem. (Isa. 66:13)

> Blessed be the God and Father of our Lord Jesus Christ, the Father of mercies and God of all comfort, who comforts us in all our tribulation, that we may be able to comfort those who are in any trouble, with the comfort with which we ourselves are comforted by God. (2 Cor. 1:3–4)

## Working It Out

So how will you handle the pain of loss? What ways have you found to comfort yourself or find comfort from others? Here are some thoughts from John:

1. *I talk to my youth pastor, Tom. He is someone I can really trust. He'll help me figure out my feelings.*
2. *Sometimes I listen to music. It is a nice way to just chill out and think about other things.*
3. *When that happened to Jack, I was so mad. I just wanted to go out and pick a fight with a tree or something. I know that isn't such a good way to comfort myself, but I felt so helpless. It would have been comforting to feel some pain for Jack.*

Now it's your turn. Take some time and consider the questions that follow as a way to think through how you will handle the pain of loss and find comfort for yourself. List five ways you have comforted yourself when you have experienced loss.

1. _____
2. _____
3. _____
4. _____
5. _____

Were these ways healthy? How about number 1?   ☐ yes   ☐ no
Number 2?   ☐ yes   ☐ no
Number 3?   ☐ yes   ☐ no
Number 4?   ☐ yes   ☐ no
Number 5?   ☐ yes   ☐ no

After thinking about healthy and unhealthy ways of finding comfort after a loss, will you change the way you respond the next time you experience a loss? How are you going to comfort yourself? Here is a list of possible alternatives. Check the ones you think you may be able to use when you need comfort:

- ☐ Talk to a friend (*Who?* _____)
- ☐ Listen to comforting (not depressing) music
- ☐ Talk to one of my parents
- ☐ Go for a walk
- ☐ Write in my journal about my loss
- ☐ Read the Bible about God's comfort (Use the verses from this section.)
- ☐ Go to a comforting place, like a park
- ☐ Do something physical (jog, play tennis, shoot hoops with a friend)
- ☐ Read how Jesus allowed Himself to cry over the loss of His friend Lazarus (See John 11.)

Take some time to consider the impact of the losses you have experienced in your life. Also, consider the things you have learned in this phase of the quest and how you can comfort yourself when faced with the pain of loss. John wrote this about what he had learned:

## Travel Log

*Wow! I never realized Dad had such painful memories or that he could possibly feel the way I do. He really had it hard when he lost his friend.*

*I have learned a lot in this part of my quest. I have learned it is OK to feel bad when I lose a friend, or even when I lose a relationship with someone, like when Jennifer and I broke up. Now I understand more about what I was feeling then. It was a lot like what I'm feeling now, except it wasn't as bad.*

*It is comforting to know that Jesus understands the pain I am in too. I guess everyone has to face loss at some point. Maybe from this experience I can be of some help to my friends if anything happens to them.*

*John*

Now it's your turn:

**Date:** _____

_____
_____
_____
_____
_____
_____
_____
_____
_____
_____
_____
_____
_____
_____
_____
_____
_____
_____
_____
_____
_____
_____
_____
_____
_____
_____
_____
_____

# Chapter Nineteen

---

# God Doubt

It was the week before finals when John was first challenged about his belief in God. He was talking to Jeff, a new friend, about studying together. They were standing outside the school, waiting for their rides home, when Jeff suggested, "Let's get together Sunday morning."

"I can't," John replied, "that's when we go to church." Every Sunday that John could remember, he and his family had piled into the car for church and Sunday school. If John asked his dad to let him study on Sunday morning he knew there would be a long lecture on the importance of church, making God the first priority, and a whole list of other reasons why the answer was no.

"You believe that stuff?" Jeff's voice indicated he had serious doubts about Christianity.

"Yeah, I guess so," John answered apologetically, a little embarrassed. He really had not thought much about his beliefs. Because he had been reared in a Christian family, he had taken for granted that most people believed the way his family did.

"I don't know, man. I don't believe in stuff I can't see," Jeff said a bit sarcastically. "Besides, if God really exists, why does so much bad stuff happen in the world?"

It was a tough question, one John hadn't seriously considered until Jeff challenged his beliefs. Until this point, John had gone through the motions of being a Christian, going to church, reading his Bible once in a while, even praying before meals and bedtime. But he had never asked himself if it really meant anything.

Ironically, the troublesome question from Jeff came at a time when John thought he was ready for anything that might happen on his quest toward adulthood. Now he was having doubts—but not the self-doubts he had felt before. He had enough confidence now to know better than to doubt himself. So what was John doubting?

Often near the middle or end of these adventurous quests another kind of doubt sneaks into the traveler's mind, "God doubt." Jeff had told John he didn't believe in things he couldn't see. Since Jeff couldn't see God, he felt he couldn't believe in Him.

One of the twelve disciples was like that, too. Thomas didn't believe Jesus had risen from the dead. He said, "Unless I see in His hands the print of the nails, and put my finger into the print of the nails, and put my hand into His side, I will not believe" (John 20:25). Obviously, Thomas, like Jeff, thought seeing was believing.

Sometimes God doubt will creep into your quest, causing you to wonder whether it makes any sense to continue. Sometimes you may doubt whether God really exists. And even if you completely believe in God's existence, you sometimes may wonder if He has the power to help with your everyday decisions or if He even knows you exist.

This is completely normal. But it's important to deal with this doubt quickly because, although there are many ways to doubt God, there is only one result: Your quest comes to a standstill. If God is not in charge of your growth into truth and maturity, then you're wasting your time. Why even bother growing up when life has no meaning or purpose?

Rather than quitting or turning back, talk to Him and ask again for His leadership and guidance. Don't let God doubt keep you from finishing this exciting adventure.

Does God exist? This is an extremely important decision; your whole future is based on what you decide. Let's look for a moment at what God has said about Himself:

- **God never changes.**
  For I am the LORD, I do not change. (Mal. 3:6)

- **God never gets tired.**
  Have you not known? Have you not heard? The everlasting God, the LORD, the Creator of the ends of the earth, neither faints nor is weary. (Isa. 40:28)

- **God is always peaceful and kind.**
  "For the mountains shall depart and the hills be removed, but My kindness shall not depart from you, nor shall My covenant of peace be removed," says the LORD, who has mercy on you. (Isa. 54:10)

- **God can do anything.**
  For with God nothing will be impossible. (Luke 1:37)

- **God knows everything.**
  Great is our Lord, and mighty in power;
  His understanding is infinite. (Ps. 147:5)

- **God is completely good.**
  Let no one say when he is tempted, "I am tempted by God"; for God cannot be tempted by evil, nor does He Himself tempt anyone. (James 1:13)

- **God is loving**
  He who does not love does not know God, for God is love. (1 John 4:8)

If, like John, you're having God doubt, here's the deal: You need to decide whether to proceed on your adventure with God, whether to try to go on without Him, or whether to quit the trip entirely. It's a question of faith, which is believing in something that can't be seen. (See Hebrews 11:1.) God is there and ready to help, but you have to have faith that He will do it when you ask. Take some time and examine how God doubt exhibits itself in your life by answering a few questions.

## Working It Out

These are some times when I have wondered if God could hear me or if He cared:

☐ I talked to Him about some problems that didn't work out
☐ My beliefs were challenged by a friend
☐ I was angry at my parents
☐ I thought God had allowed something bad happen to me or to someone else
☐ I prayed and didn't feel anything
☐ I prayed about a boyfriend or girlfriend and the relationship didn't work out
☐ I had a problem and God didn't take it away
☐ I tried out for something (a sports team, the school play) and God didn't let me make it
☐ I prayed about a test and did badly
☐ (Other) _____

In each of the situations above, why did you doubt God? (Think about the above list and write why you believe God didn't rescue you or make things better in each situation you checked.)

1. _____
_____
2. _____
_____
3. _____
_____
4. _____
_____
5. _____
_____

Check the possible events that might occur in your future that could cause you to doubt God:

☐ Seeing people say they are Christians but act like they're not
☐ Watching my family pray and still have to struggle with things
☐ Being tempted to do things I know aren't Christian, like drugs or sex
☐ Not being able to see proof of God's existence
☐ Getting bored trying to lead a good life
☐ Wondering if other religions might be real and Christianity might not be
☐ Having friends make fun of me for being a Christian
☐ Sometimes wanting to rebel when my family insists I go to church
☐ Not having my questions about God taken seriously
☐ (Other) _____
_____

How could what you just learned about who God is change the way you feel about Him in times of potential doubt?

☐ I will trust Him more
☐ I will believe in His goodness and kindness
☐ I will remember that He loves and cares about me
☐ I know He can do anything so there's no reason to doubt His power
☐ I have discovered He never changes, so I can believe He will always be there for me
☐ I realize He doesn't get tired, so He's always ready to help when I need Him

☐ I understand that He won't tempt me to do wrong
☐ I can see that God wants only the best for me
☐ I found out God is stronger than any of my problems
☐ (Other) _____

Make a plan for how you will handle God doubt when it occurs in the future (as it certainly will). Check the boxes that apply to you, then write out your plan in the space provided.

☐ I will read the verses on who God says He is
☐ I will pray and ask God's help with my doubt
☐ I will avoid letting my doubts keep me from completing my quest
☐ I will make a list of reasons why I am having doubts and share them with someone
☐ I will talk to my (circle those that apply):

| | | |
|---|---|---|
| Pastor | Christian friend(s) | Teacher |
| Youth leader | Mom or Dad | Coach |
| Counselor | Grandparent | (Other) _____ |

☐ (Other) _____

Now, write out the plan you have just developed.

When God doubt starts bothering me, I will: _____

_____

_____

_____

_____

_____

Everyone on this quest will go through times of doubt and questioning sometimes. So that you know what to do when that happens, write down your thoughts, feelings, and questions about this topic in your Travel Log. If you still have lots of questions about God, make it a point to talk to someone who can help—your pastor, parents, or someone else you trust.

# Chapter Twenty

## I Feel So Bored!

**T**here must be something wrong with me, Beth thought. It's Friday night and I'm sitting here alone in my room.

An incredibly restless feeling was developing deep within her. She played her favorite tape and turned it up loud, trying to drown out the feeling that something just wasn't right. After a few minutes she turned it off and picked up a magazine. But after scanning the page for a few minutes, Beth threw the magazine to the floor. She moved to the TV room, hoping to find an interesting show. The restless feeling gnawed away at her insides as she flipped through the channels.

Beth felt as though her life was at a standstill and nothing she did could make it better. The harder she tried, the more bored, empty, and frustrated she seemed to feel. It was a long evening.

While adolescence is usually full of hurried activity, there are times when it all appears to come screeching to an abrupt halt. During those momentary stops, a lot of things can happen.

Let's return to our analogy of a long hike through the mountains. You know when you finally arrive at the end of the trip the excitement will be tremendous. But that seems a long way off. Right now it seems you're just seeing the same old stuff along the trail—trees, rocks, wildlife. You've been watching your steps to avoid hidden dangers, but for a long time now there have been none. It's getting quite boring.

Experienced hikers on long mountain trips are familiar with this experience. It was exciting when they started the long trek, and they know the rush at the end will be thrilling. There's even some neat stuff in the middle. But sometimes the miles upon miles of constant climbing can seem to stretch on endlessly, and the climbers start to feel as if they're not even moving forward anymore.

That is just what Beth was experiencing. Her quest had lost its excitement and she believed this was a sign that something wasn't quite right with her. This feeling of boredom can be quite intense. Actually, though, a bit of boredom once in a while is quite normal. Our lives must slow down sometimes, or we would become totally exhausted. Not everyone realizes this, however; some people think that boredom indicates that something is wrong.

For example, Beth assumed her Friday-night boredom happened because she was unpopular or incredibly dull. She believed the boredom was something she was born with, rather than a normal part of the growth process. She tried to think of ways to overcome her problem.

One solution she thought about was trying to completely change herself so she would become more interesting to others. (Actually, others would probably have seen through the changes and considered her a fake.) Another solution, she thought miserably, would be to give up and stay miserable, accepting that as just the way God made her.

When they're bored, some teenagers rush the maturing process, trying to make it happen faster. Adolescents often start smoking because they believe a cigarette makes them look and feel more mature. Others try drinking and/or using drugs for the same reason. Still others try sex, believing it will make them a "real" man or woman. In fact, there are lots of adult behaviors you can try to make yourself look older or more mature. But the truth is, the behaviors don't make you mature any more than sitting in a garage making motor sounds makes you an automobile. It's not the outward behaviors, it's the inner attitudes that prove you're mature.

Another type of person may try thrill-seeking behaviors to fight boredom. Some of these behaviors can be dangerous, like speeding in a car, running away from home, fighting, or even breaking the law. In the short run, the boredom may disappear, but the thrill-seeking can lead you far down a side path, away from the main trail. And as you know, it can be very difficult finding your way back.

Each of these reactions to boredom is similar in one important way: Each assumes there's something wrong and action is needed to change the boredom. But usually, that's not the case. The simple truth is that growing up takes time, and during that time there will be periods of excitement, as well as boredom. It's all part of the quest.

Stop trying to look for alternative routes or shortcuts. These only lead away from the main trail of growth and truth and make the journey longer because you have to find your way back to where you got off.

Everyone gets bored sometimes, so don't worry when it happens to you. At those times remember that God is slowly, patiently, and ever-so-carefully forming you into an adult who knows how to cope with life, including the difficult times that may lie ahead. Boredom is just part of the quest. Be patient with yourself—and with God as He does His work in you.

## Working It Out

Some of the times when I've been bored by how long it takes to grow up are:

- ☐ Today
- ☐ Yesterday
- ☐ Last week
- ☐ A weekend when there was nothing to do
- ☐ Waiting for my sixteenth birthday so I could drive
- ☐ Most of the days at school
- ☐ The days when my parents treat me like a child
- ☐ I'm almost always bored
- ☐ (Other) _____

In these times I usually reacted by:

- ☐ Trying something new to seem more mature
- ☐ Looking for excitement and kicks
- ☐ Blaming myself for being a dull, boring person
- ☐ Searching for a new relationship to fill the emptiness
- ☐ Blaming my boredom on others
- ☐ Thinking something was really wrong
- ☐ Sitting around doing nothing and feeling rotten
- ☐ (Other) _____

When I feel bored inside, I:

☐ Tell myself life isn't fair
☐ Feel I need to do something *right now*
☐ Ask myself why it is always me who gets bored
☐ Feel nobody likes me
☐ Feel I'm a loser
☐ Tell myself I hate my life
☐ Feel depressed
☐ Start thinking everyone else has it better than I do
☐ (Other) _____

Instead, next time I feel bored and empty inside, I can tell myself:

☐ It's OK; growth takes time
☐ God is still working on changing me
☐ Be patient; things will get better
☐ This is normal
☐ Relax; use the time to rest
☐ There's no need to do anything
☐ (Other) _____

Some healthy things I can do in the future to cope with my boredom are:

☐ Get a new hobby
☐ Exercise
☐ Read a book
☐ Review what I've learned from my quest
☐ Write a letter
☐ Call an old friend I haven't seen in a while
☐ Do an unexpected favor
☐ Talk with my parents
☐ (Other) _____

# Chapter
# Twenty-one

---

# Bitterness and
# Forgiveness

*Sometimes I get so mad that I just don't know what to do with all my anger. Just an hour ago my mom started ragging on my friends again. She was asking about their future plans, whether they are Christians, if they smoke and drink. It seems like she's always treating me like a kid. Will she ever trust me enough to let me grow up?*

*I stomped out of the house and slammed the back door. I walked around the neighborhood for a while and cooled off a little bit, but I still felt pretty mad. It sort of builds up and I just don't know what to do. And it's not just that. It seems like I'm always angry at her. I know I should apologize and try to make things*

*right but I just don't feel like it. Maybe if she would apologize to
me first things would feel better. What should I do?*
*John*

You have the right to be angry when someone harms you or wrongs
you. But sometimes anger may build up inside you and you have no idea
how to let it go. So you may try to forget and pretend nothing is wrong—
until the next time an argument or disagreement happens; then the anger
pops up again, stronger than ever, and you feel like you're going to explode.
That built-up anger is bitterness. When you forgive the person who has
caused you to feel angry, you release the pressure and prevent bitterness from
building.

You're probably thinking that by forgiveness we also mean forgetting.
But when something makes you really angry, it seems almost impossible to
forget it, right? Actually, forgiving and forgetting are two separate things. Let
us explain. Often, long after an injury has healed, there is still a scar; it may
even last the rest of your life. It's there, but it doesn't hurt anymore.

Similarly, when someone wrongs you, it creates an emotional wound.
When you forgive the person who wronged you, that injury also heals, leaving behind a psychological scar. It reminds you of the situation that made
you so angry, but you don't feel the anger and pain anymore.

On the other hand, when you fail to forgive, and keep holding on to
bitterness and anger, the emotional wound doesn't have a chance to heal. As
long as the bitter feelings last, the sore stays open and painful. The only way
to begin the healing is to forgive.

This leaves you with a choice. You can either allow healing to begin
by starting the forgiveness process, or you can choose to stay bitter and angry. If you choose to continue being angry, you saddle yourself with a painful burden that weighs you down with bitterness and keeps you from being
free to do the important work of maturing.

Some bitter people make the situation worse by constantly thinking of
ways to get revenge. Sometimes this vengefulness becomes more important
than anything else; their lives are dominated by thoughts of how to make the
others pay for the wrongs they have done. When you think about it, having
such an all-consuming goal means the angry ones are being controlled by
the other persons. The others' actions determine how the angry persons will
behave.

In contrast, some people keep their anger inside. They pretend nothing's wrong, but the anger keeps building. Because they fail to deal with it directly, their anger eventually turns inward. They become angry at themselves, and if they don't find a healthy way to relieve the anger, they may start injuring themselves or even consider killing themselves.

Faced with these possible consequences, you can probably see why it's better to forgive than to allow anger and bitterness to control your life. Paul emphasized the importance of this concept when he wrote, "Let all bitterness, wrath, anger, clamor, and evil speaking be put away from you, with all malice. And be kind to one another, tenderhearted, forgiving one another, just as God in Christ also forgave you" (Eph. 4:31–32).

Now you're probably saying, "OK, but how do I go about this forgiving stuff?" Your anger may have been building for quite some time, and now you find it hard to be in the same place with the person who wronged you. So you start avoiding him or her, even if it means not doing something you would otherwise enjoy. See how your anger affects you?

The first step in forgiving is understanding why you should let the other person "off the hook." It may be easier to approach this from another perspective: While forgiveness may let the other person off the hook, the real benefit is that it frees *you* also. It relieves you of the bitterness and anger that are weighing you down, keeping you from doing things you would like to and occupying time you could use for other things. Look at the situation this way and you'll see that the bitterness and anger you are feeling are just not worth the burden they cause. When you realize this, you are ready to forgive.

The next step is asking God to soften your heart so it's easier to let go of the bitterness you are holding so tightly. When you ask for God's help, you might even find that this person's actions or words bug you so much because they're the same kinds of things you've said or done yourself, and you know they've caused problems for you. By understanding that you are not perfect either and may have made similar mistakes, you will be ready to approach the other person to talk about what is bugging you.

That's the final stage of forgiveness, talking directly to the person you feel has wronged you. Calmly and earnestly try to tell him or her exactly how you feel about what is happening between you and describe how it has been weighing you down and harming your relationship. Then let the other person know you want to forgive him or her and get the problem out of the path of your growth and maturity.

We know this won't be easy. In fact, it may require lots of thinking, prayer, and work. But keep telling yourself you forgive him or her and refuse to feel bitter and angry. Remember what Jesus told Peter when he asked how many times he should forgive someone who wronged him. Jesus answered, "I do not say to you, up to seven times, but up to seventy times seven" (Matt. 18:22). Forgiving once may not be enough; you may have to keep forgiving.

You don't have to go through life being bitter and angry, holding grudges, and getting revenge for wrongs people have done to you. You have the choice to forgive and get the burden off your back. Forgiveness is a choice you make so your life can be better. Only you can make that decision.

Here's your chance to look at bitterness in your own life and find opportunities to work on forgiveness. Take some time and answer the questions below.

## Working It Out

List some situations when you felt angry and bitter. John wrote:

1. *When my parents constantly judge my friends.*
2. *When my parents don't trust me, even when I'm trying my hardest.*
3. *When Coach Briggs puts me down in front of the team for making a bad play.*

Now list some of your own:

1. _____
2. _____
3. _____

How have the situations below weighed you down and kept you from completing your quest? John replied:

*When my parents judge my friends it makes me want to choose bad ones just to get them back. When my parents won't trust me I stop caring and do stuff I know is wrong. When Coach Briggs puts me down I get angry and mess up worse next time.*

How about you?

_____
_____
_____
_____
_____
_____

Check off reasons why you stay bitter instead of forgiving and letting go.

☐ I don't want others to think I'm weak
☐ It's easier to be angry than to forgive
☐ I don't want to let others off the hook after they have hurt me
☐ Sometimes I'm stubborn and I show it by staying angry
☐ When I hold on to the anger, I feel like I'm in control of the situation
☐ I make people feel bad by being angry, and that pays them back for hurt-
ing me
☐ (Other) _____

It's important to have a plan for forgiving people; otherwise you risk letting your anger get in the way of your quest. Here is John's plan:

_First I can pray and ask God to soften my bitterness and show me how to approach the situation. I could even talk to my youth pastor, Tom, about it. Then I could ask my parents to spend a few minutes alone with me sometime this week so we can talk about it, and I could talk to Coach Briggs after practice. I should write down what I plan to say so that I don't unintentionally say stuff to make the situation worse._

Now create a plan of your own:

_____
_____
_____
_____
_____
_____

A very important part of growing up is learning how to forgive. Many adults have never learned how to do this; they go through life bitter and angry about old situations they have never worked out. This is dangerous because it can carry over into other relationships later on. The only way past this obstacle in your path is taking time to forgive and getting rid of the burden that weighs you down.

# Chapter Twenty-two

## The Canyon

It had been a great day but an exhausting one. Now Beth and the kids in the church youth group were wearily enduring the bus ride back home from Thrills Galore, a huge amusement park two hours' ride from home.

When Beth's friend Sheila had invited her to go, Beth had hesitated, thinking the other kids would hit on her right from the start with "God stuff." She was surprised, though. The kids seemed a lot like her.

The day was really fun, with lots of food, rides, and getting acquainted. The person who stood out the most to Beth, though, wasn't a kid. She was the youth pastor's wife, Jan.

*She seems so real,* Beth thought, *like someone who isn't afraid to let people see who she really is.* Jan was also warm, kind, and fun to be with. On the way home the bus was pretty quiet. Some kids had sacked out, with their heads bobbing against the windows. Beth made her way toward Jan.

"Could I talk to you a minute?" Beth asked. Jan looked up with a smile; she didn't seem surprised to see Beth standing there.

"Sure, sit down. Tell me what's on your mind. I noticed that something was bothering you all day. You do a pretty good job of hiding it, but not that good." Beth was impressed that someone actually had taken enough interest in her to notice she wasn't all that happy.

"Jan, you seem so confident and sure of yourself. How do you do it?" Beth thought she would start with something easy before jumping in too quick with her real questions.

"Oh, I don't know. I guess I learned a few things through my years of growing up that helped me to be at ease with myself." Jan did seem calm and relaxed.

Beth took a big breath, then plunged ahead. "Jan, I've been feeling so empty lately. I guess I feel so insignificant and directionless. It feels like I don't have anything to live for. Don't get me wrong. I'm not suicidal or anything. It's just that I don't seem to have any purpose in my life. It feels like I just don't matter and no one really cares."

"I felt that way, too, Beth, at one time," Jan answered. "It seemed like nothing really satisfied me, and I felt like I was looking for something but I didn't know what it was."

"That's exactly how I feel!" Beth confessed. "Nothing seems to make any difference sometimes. How did you ever it figure out?"

"I did just what you're doing. I watched that person to see if she lived what she talked. Then I sat down and talked with her." Jan hesitated, gathering her thoughts.

"Don't give up yet, Beth. There's an answer, but it isn't found in things. It is found in a Person—and that Person is Jesus. Through a relationship with Jesus Christ, I found meaning for my life and the ability to accept myself without getting all hung up on the things I couldn't do."

At any other time, Beth would have said "Thanks," and walked away. She didn't want a cliché as an answer. She needed something real. But something about the way Jan's eyes sparkled when she spoke made Beth want to know more.

"So, where does the meaning come from?" she asked slowly.

"It comes from my understanding of just how much God loves me," Jan said. "The Bible says in John 3:16, 'For God so loved the world that He gave His only begotten Son, that whoever believes in Him should not perish but have everlasting life.' It takes a tremendous amount of love to give up someone you love to save people who don't even know you exist."

"Yeah, I can't even imagine that." Beth had never heard it put this way before.

"Think about this: We were created to have a relationship with God and to find our purpose in that relationship. And God's ultimate desire was to have a relationship with you and me. Here, Beth, let me show you what I mean." Jan got her Bible out of her backpack and flipped through the pages. "Here, you read it," she said, pointing to Colossians 1:16.

Beth hesitated a moment. Then her eyes started moving over the words: "For by Him all things were created that are in heaven and that are on earth, visible and invisible, whether thrones or dominions or principalities or powers. All things were created through Him and for Him."

When she finished, she looked at Jan. "God created us for Himself? Why?"

"Because He wanted to have a relationship with us," Jan said with a smile.

"Oh."

"But there was a problem," Jan continued. "In the Garden of Eden, Adam and Eve turned their backs on God by disobeying Him. We have all inherited that same rebellious spirit. So you can see the 'predicament' God was in. He wanted a relationship with us, but He couldn't tolerate our sinfulness. He had to find some way to restore this relationship with us. That way came in the person of Jesus Christ. Are you beginning to see the picture?"

"Yes, it is beginning to make sense," Beth answered. "God wanted a relationship with us, but we sort of ignored that and did what we wanted—which separated us forever from Him since He couldn't tolerate sin."

"Right! Jesus was the solution to that problem. He died as a substitute for us by paying the death penalty we deserved for our rebellion. That wasn't the end of it, though. He not only died but He overcame death and rose again. And since He did, He is still alive to give us a new opportunity to have that relationship with God. The only thing that is left is whether we respond to that opportunity God gives us in Jesus."

A sense of hope stirred deep within Beth's spirit. "Jan, what can I do?"

"There are three things you must do, Beth. First, you must repent of your rebellion and sinfulness. Second, you must believe that Jesus died for your sins to provide forgiveness and a new relationship with God. Finally, you must decide to receive Christ as Your Savior and Lord with the intent to obey Him. In Revelation 3:20, Jesus said, 'Behold, I stand at the door and knock. If anyone hears My voice and opens the door, I will come in to him and dine with him, and he with Me.' That means if you accept the free gift God provides you, He will establish a relationship with you that will give you eternal life and guarantee your eternal relationship with Him in heaven."

"Jan, I want that. Tell me what to do."

"Let's pray, Beth."

Beth prayed with Jan that night and accepted Jesus as her Lord and Savior. Her life didn't change overnight, but she did sense a new beginning.

The deep, empty canyon you face in your quest—a huge, yawning hole that splits the trail far below—represents the same emptiness Beth experienced. That canyon is a black and empty chasm that chills your heart. You stare a little harder. *There is no bridge.*

God offers you a way across this dark canyon of despair and emptiness. That way is a relationship with Jesus Christ. Accepting this gift means you put your faith in Jesus for eternal life. By making this decision, you admit that you are unable to control your life as you want. You can try to keep your independence and cross the canyon on your own, or you can surrender your life to Jesus, the One who offers the significance and meaning you long for. The choice is yours.

## Working It Out

Do you think you have what it takes to cross the canyon of emptiness alone?   ☐ yes   ☐ no

What will you do?

☐ Accept the gift of a relationship that God offers me in Jesus Christ
☐ Reaffirm myself to the decision I made long ago about my relationship with Jesus
☐ Nothing. I am strong enough to handle the challenges of growing up by myself

Check some of the things you worry about as you consider where your life might be headed in the future:

☐ How will my friends respond to the new changes in my life?
☐ Will my parents expect more of me now as I mature?
☐ Will I be able to handle the responsibilities of adulthood?

☐ Am I strong enough to begin separating from my family?
☐ What if my family resists letting me take on responsibility for my own decisions?
☐ Will I make the wrong choices and end up worse than before?
☐ If I mess up too much will God get disgusted and turn His back on me?
☐ (Other) _____

How has your quest prepared you to handle worries like those you've just checked?

☐ I've learned to trust God to lead me, rather than relying too much on myself
☐ I know how to make better decisions than I did before
☐ I've realized I can get through "impossible" times
☐ I understand the importance of asking for help when I don't have answers
☐ I know myself better than I did before
☐ I've learned to travel one step at a time rather than worrying about the future
☐ I now understand that no problem is too big for God to handle
☐ (Other) _____

# PART THREE

## The Summit

# Chapter Twenty-three

---

## Rites of Passage

**Y**ou have completed the quest on which you have embarked, and now you stand at the end—and at a beginning. You're about to step through a doorway, a passage, that is symbolic of so many other experiences you will face throughout your life. Take graduation from high school, for example. In many areas, it is called "commencement." At first, that might seem like a strange word to describe the end of your high school education. But of course it's less an end than a beginning, the beginning of a new period of growth and development in your life.

Different cultures throughout history have developed rituals, or rites, to celebrate a person's passage from one stage of life into another. Some of these cultures have given their young people a way to symbolize the step from childhood into adulthood.

One of John's friends had gone through something like that. Ben Levine was a lot younger than John, but they shared an interest in basketball, and Ben was a pretty good ball player for his age. They would often get together to shoot baskets and talk. During one of those talks, Ben told John about his *bar mitzvah*.

"All the family was there. It was a fun time," Ben said.

"What does that mean, *bar mitzvah*? I've never heard of that," John said.

Ben answered, "Well, you know I'm Jewish, right? In our family and culture, on the first Sabbath after a boy passes his twelfth birthday, his father takes him to the synagogue—like your church—where he is called 'A Son of the Law.' That's what my dad and I did."

"Is that all there is to it?" John asked.

"Oh no. There were some other parts of the ceremony that are hard to explain. But some of it is easier to understand. My dad said a prayer for me, and he said, 'Blessed be thou, O God, who has taken from me the responsibility for this boy.' Then I prayed, 'O my God and God of my fathers! On this solemn and sacred day, which marks my passage from boyhood to manhood, I humbly raise my eyes unto thee, and declare with sincerity and truth that henceforth I will keep thy commandments, and undertake and bear the responsibility of my actions toward thee,'" Ben said.

"Wow, that sounds like some ceremony. What does it all mean?"

"It means that after my *bar mitzvah*, I am considered an adult in the synagogue. I can practice Judaism as an adult, and I am responsible for observing the Torah, or law, and I can participate in the activities of the synagogue."

For Ben, there was a clear dividing line in his life; almost overnight he became a man and was given the rights and responsibilities of adulthood. Obviously, the rite of passage doesn't actually transform a child into an adult, but it is a way of marking the end of childhood and the beginning of adulthood.

In ancient Greece, a boy was under his father's care from age seven until he was eighteen. He then became what was called a cadet, and for two years he was under the direction of the state. The Athenians were divided into ten clans. Before a boy became a cadet he was received into a clan, and as a ceremonial act his long hair was cut off and offered to the gods. Once again, growing up was marked by specific events.

Under Roman law the year at which a boy grew up was not definitely fixed, but it was always between the ages of fourteen and seventeen. At a sacred festival in the family, he took off the toga worn by children (which had a narrow band of purple at the hem) and put on the plain white toga of the adults. He was then conducted by his friends and relatives down to the forum (a place where the adults gathered to decide community issues). There he was formally introduced to public life. A Roman custom dictated that on the day a child "grew up" a boy offered his ball and a girl offered her doll to Apollo to show they had put away childish things.

The apostle Paul referred to the change from childhood into adulthood as a transforming event. Here is how Paul put it:

> When I was a child, I spoke as a child, I understood as a child, I thought as a child; but when I became a man, I put away childish things.
> (1 Cor. 13:11)

> Now I say that the heir, as long as he is a child, does not differ at all from a slave, though he is master of all. (Gal. 4:1)

When you come of age and become an adult in others' eyes you put childish ways behind you (such as expecting others to make your decisions for you or following your peers without using your own judgment about what is right).

As you grow in adulthood, you also gain the privilege of freedom. That means you have greater choices about what you will do—and you, alone, will bear the consequences of those choices.

The ability to handle the privilege of freedom without abusing it means you're also gaining responsibility. That is another indication of others' acceptance of you as an emerging adult—the gradual transfer of responsibility from your parents to you. This responsibility can be an awesome burden, and it is not to be taken lightly. It might be a burden you would like to share. Christ is more than sufficient to help you with this. Remember what He said about His yoke being easy and His burden light? He will share the load with you, helping you bear the responsibility for yourself.

## Working It Out

What does it mean to you to have freedom?
(John wrote, *I always thought that having freedom meant that I could do what I wanted, when I wanted to.*)

_____

_____

_____

Name three "childish ways" you can give up to mark your passage into adulthood. (We included some of John's responses to help you.)

1. I can take no for an answer from my parents. When I fight with them, I'm being childish about not getting my way.
2. I can choose to do things that are good for me (even when it looks like what my parents want). The important thing is that I chose it, not my parents.
3. When my parents extend my curfew, I can stick with it. That will prove I am worthy of being considered an adult because that is what an adult would do.

OK, now it's your turn.

1. _____
   _____
   _____
2. _____
   _____
   _____
3. _____
   _____
   _____

# Chapter
# Twenty-four

---

# Worthy of
# Adulthood

Congratulations on the completion of your quest! Finally, the time of passing has come. You are on the threshold of a new beginning as an adult.

You have come to understand that becoming an adult is something that is proven, not just given to you. Your behavior and the decisions you make will be the sure proof of whether or not you are an adult.

This status is granted based on how you act under pressure, not just when things are easy. After all, anyone can be adult-like when there is no pressure. (Even kids can do that!) It is in the pressure-filled situations, such as when your peers are pushing you to go against your values or you are tempted to violate your curfew or you are tempted to drink, that the people around you will see whether you are an adult or a child.

Oh, to be sure, by your body size and physical appearance you may be an adult. But are you an emotional adult by the decisions you make, or even how you make them? These are all critical questions to consider if you think you are worthy of adulthood.

The Bible talks a lot about worthiness, particularly in terms of how someone conducts himself in light of his commitment to Jesus Christ. Here are just a few verses that show you what we mean:

> That you may walk worthy of the Lord, fully pleasing Him, being fruitful in every good work and increasing in the knowledge of God. (Col. 1:10)

> That you would walk worthy of God who calls you into His own kingdom and glory. (1 Thess. 2:12)

Worthiness means that you are "walking the talk" of the Christian life, doing what you say you believe. Remember what drew Beth to Jan, the youth pastor's wife? It was the consistency by which Jan lived her life. It was attractive and refreshing to Beth to see this woman live out her beliefs.

That kind of consistency carries over into your life as an adult. There will be times when the people around you—even your parents—may not act like adults, but that is no excuse to lapse into child-like behavior yourself. Remember that it won't always be easy to be an adult. It takes a lot of work to "walk the talk" of adulthood.

While we urge you to set high standards for yourself, we offer one last one caution. Don't be too hard on yourself and don't expect perfection.

You will have relapses along the way. Everyone does. Difficult situations can bring out the child in all of us. But even in those times, it is more adult-like to admit your weakness than to act like nothing is wrong. Live life honestly before God and others, and you will accomplish what you have set out to do—grow and mature.

We hope you never stop growing, learning, loving, caring for others, and maturing in Christ. It is a process that continues as long as you live. We hope that at the end of your life's journey you can say to God, as the apostle Paul did, "I have fought the good fight, I have finished the race, I have kept the faith" (2 Tim. 4:7).

Here are some more wise words from the apostle Paul to take along on your journey:

> Not that I have already attained, or am already perfected; but I press on, that I may lay hold of that for which Christ Jesus has also laid hold of me. Brethren, I do not count myself to have apprehended; but one thing I do, forgetting those things which are behind and reaching forward to those things which are ahead, I press toward the goal for the prize of the upward call of God in Christ Jesus. (Phil. 3:12–14)

Take along these thoughts, too:

- The price of greatness is responsibility. *Winston Churchill*

- No man is worth his salt who is not ready at all times to risk his body, to risk his well-being, to risk his life, in a great cause.
  *Theodore Roosevelt*

- We must develop and maintain the capacity to forgive. He who is devoid of the power to forgive is devoid of the power to love.
  *Martin Luther King*

- You cannot help men permanently by doing for them what they could and should do for themselves. *Abraham Lincoln*

Write your thoughts and feelings about your worthiness to be an adult. To get you started, we'll take one last look at what Beth and John wrote:

## Travel Log

*Well, I guess this is it. I have come to the end of my quest, and now I begin a new life of adulthood. It is sad to leave childhood and adolescence behind. I feel like I'm losing something, even though it is exciting and exhilarating to be considered an adult. I feel a loss in leaving the security of childhood behind. It was nice to have my parents always there when I needed them. That's not to say they are not going to be there in the future, but it will be different. The situation I find myself in will still be mine to cope with, even with their help. It feels a little lonely, but I guess that is to be expected. More than loneliness about leaving my childhood, though, I feel excitement and confidence about the future that lies ahead.*

*Beth*

*The end has finally come. I don't understand why I feel so sad. I was sure I was going to be overjoyed to see this come to an end. But that isn't the case. I have learned a lot about myself—my strengths and my weaknesses. I have been surprised to find myself becoming comfortable with my shortcomings because I think I have finally understood that God accepts me, no matter what. That makes it a little easier for me to accept myself. I need to always remind myself that it isn't bad to be weak. It is in my weakness that God will show His strength in my life. That is what I want. Sometimes I'm not sure I am really ready to become an adult as it has been talked about in* The Quest, *but with God's help I will try to keep pressing on.*

*John*

Now it's your turn:

**Date:** _____

_____

_____

_____

_____

_____

_____

_____

_____

_____

_____

_____

_____

_____

_____

_____

_____

_____

_____

_____

_____

_____

_____

_____

_____

_____

_____

_____

_____

_____

_____

# about the authors

**Kevin Brown** is a psychotherapist and program director of the adolescent inpatient hospital program at the Minirth-Meier Clinic in Wheaton, Illinois. He specializes in the treatment of abusive families and those recovering from traumatic relationships. He received his M.S.W. from the University of Illinois at Chicago and his B.A. from Wheaton College. Brown and his wife, Sandy, and son, Seth, live in the Chicago area.

**Raymond Mitsch, Ph.D.,** is a clinical psychologist and the director of the child and adolescent division of the Minirth-Meier Clinic in Wheaton. Dr. Mitsch received his M.A. and Ph.D. in counseling psychology from Indiana State University, and his B.A. from Wabash College in Crawfordsville, Indiana. He served as staff psychologist for Michigan Technological University Counseling Services for two years before moving to the Minirth-Meier Clinic in Wheaton. Dr. Mitsch, his wife, Linda, and their three children, Corrie, Anne and Abigail, live in Wheaton.

For general information about the Minirth Meier Clinic branch offices, counseling services, educational resources, and hospital programs, call toll-free 1-800-545-1819.